Y0-CUN-109

Wake Technical Community College
9101 Fayetteville Road
Raleigh, North Carolina 27603

people in the NEWS

Wake Technical Community College
9101 Fayetteville Road
Raleigh, North Carolina 27603

Cristiano Ronaldo

by Gail B. Stewart

LUCENT BOOKS
A part of Gale, Cengage Learning

GALE CENGAGE Learning

Farmington Hills, Mich • San Francisco • New York • Waterville, Maine
Meriden, Conn • Mason, Ohio • Chicago

GALE
CENGAGE Learning

© 2015 Gale, Cengage Learning

WCN:01-100-101

ALL RIGHTS RESERVED. No part of this work covered by the copyright herein may be reproduced, transmitted, stored, or used in any form or by any means graphic, electronic, or mechanical, including but not limited to photocopying, recording, scanning, digitizing, taping, Web distribution, information networks, or information storage and retrieval systems, except as permitted under Section 107 or 108 of the 1976 United States Copyright Act, without the prior written permission of the publisher.

Every effort has been made to trace the owners of copyrighted material.

LIBRARY OF CONGRESS CATALOGING-IN-PUBLICATION DATA

Stewart, Gail B. (Gail Barbara), 1949-
 Cristiano Ronaldo / by Gail B. Stewart.
   pages cm. -- (People in the News)
 Includes bibliographical references and index.
 ISBN 978-1-4205-1328-8 (hardcover)
 1. Ronaldo, Cristiano, 1985- 2. Soccer players--Portugal--Biography.
 I. Title.
 GV942.7.R626S84 2015
 796.334092--dc23
 [B]
                              2015007393

Lucent Books
27500 Drake Rd.
Farmington Hills, MI 48331

ISBN-13: 978-1-4205-1328-8
ISBN-10: 1-4205-1328-1

Printed in the United States of America
1 2 3 4 5 6 7 19 18 17 16 15

Contents

Foreword	**4**
Introduction	**6**
"The Very, Very Best in the World"	
Chapter 1	**11**
An Island Childhood	
Chapter 2	**26**
Club Soccer	
Chapter 3	**42**
The Most Expensive Teenager in Britain	
Chapter 4	**60**
A Move to Spain	
Chapter 5	**75**
Expanding His Reach	
Notes	**91**
Important Dates	**96**
For More Information	**98**
Index	**100**
Picture Credits	**104**
About the Author	**104**

Foreword

Fame and celebrity are alluring. People are drawn to those who walk in fame's spotlight, whether they are known for great accomplishments or for notorious deeds. The lives of the famous pique public interest and attract attention, perhaps because their experiences seem in some ways so different from, yet in other ways so similar to, our own.

Newspapers, magazines, and television regularly capitalize on this fascination with celebrity by running profiles of famous people. For example, television programs such as *Entertainment Tonight* devote all their programming to stories about entertainment and entertainers. Magazines such as *People* fill their pages with stories of the private lives of famous people. Even newspapers, newsmagazines, and television news frequently delve into the lives of well-known personalities. Despite the number of articles and programs, few provide more than a superficial glimpse at their subjects.

Lucent's People in the News series offers young readers a deeper look into the lives of today's newsmakers, the influences that have shaped them, and the impact they have had in their fields of endeavor and on other people's lives. The subjects of the series hail from many disciplines and walks of life. They include authors, musicians, athletes, political leaders, entertainers, entrepreneurs, and others who have made a mark on modern life and who, in many cases, will continue to do so for years to come.

These biographies are more than factual chronicles. Each book emphasizes the contributions, accomplishments, or deeds that have brought fame or notoriety to the individual and shows how that person has influenced modern life. Authors portray their subjects in a realistic, unsentimental light. For example, Bill Gates—cofounder of the software giant Microsoft—has been instrumental in making personal computers the most vital tool of the modern age. Few dispute his business savvy, his perseverance, or his technical expertise, yet critics say he is ruthless in his dealings with competitors and driven more by his desire to maintain Microsoft's dominance in the computer industry than by an interest in furthering technology.

In these books, young readers will encounter inspiring stories about real people who achieved success despite enormous obstacles. Oprah Winfrey—one of the most powerful, most watched, and wealthiest women in television history—spent the first six years of her life in the care of her grandparents while her unwed mother sought work and a better life elsewhere. Her adolescence was colored by pregnancy at age fourteen, rape, and sexual abuse.

Each author documents and supports his or her work with an array of primary and secondary source quotations taken from diaries, letters, speeches, and interviews. All quotes are footnoted to show readers exactly how and where biographers derive their information and provide guidance for further research. The quotations enliven the text by giving readers eyewitness views of the life and accomplishments of each person covered in the People in the News series.

In addition, each book in the series includes photographs, annotated bibliographies, timelines, and comprehensive indexes. For both the casual reader and the student researcher, the People in the News series offers insight into the lives of today's newsmakers—people who shape the way we live, work, and play in the modern age.

Introduction

"The Very, Very Best in the World"

On November 19, 2013, the majority of the fifty thousand spectators at Friends Arena in northern Sweden were the home fans wearing their national colors of yellow and bright blue. They waved scarves around in the air, sported Viking helmets, and sang songs to urge the Swedish soccer team to victory in this World Cup Qualifying match. They also knew how to heckle—and their favorite target was Cristiano Ronaldo, the Portugal team's most dangerous scorer.

In Ronaldo's case, the fans loved to taunt him by singing the name of Lionel Messi, the Argentinean superstar who has often been perceived as Ronaldo's rival. Such taunting had gotten under his skin in the past and had made him lose his composure during a game. The Swedes were hoping he would become flustered on this day and would be less likely to score a goal.

The tall, dark-haired Ronaldo fired a shot at the goal, but it went too high. As he grimaced in disappointment, the home fans in Sweden began to taunt and boo the Portuguese star by chanting, "Messi! Messi!!"

High Stakes

The stakes of this game were high. As soccer fans know, the World Cup is an international soccer tournament that is held only once every four years. Of all the countries in the world, only the thirty-two best are allowed in the World Cup com-

Cristiano Ronaldo (right) and Mikael Lustig vie for the ball during the FIFA 2014 World Cup qualifier match between Portugal and Sweden on November 15, 2013.

petition, making the trophy the most coveted award in all of sports.

Every nation has the chance to be a part of the tournament by playing against other countries in their region prior to the actual competition. This is known as World Cup Qualifying, and its process spans over two and a half years. In the European region, fifty-three countries were competing for thirteen available spots. The countries are divided among nine groups, which then played against one another.

The first-place country from each of the nine groups was given a spot in the next round of the 2014 World Cup in Brazil, while the second-place team in each group was forced to play a tiebreaker with another second-place team—one game at home and the other away. If each team wins one, the team with the higher number of goals scored in the two games advances. And if the number of goals is a tie, the last resort is a shoot-out. Portugal and Sweden were chosen to play against one another, and the loser of the match would have to stay home and wait another four years to try to qualify for the 2018 World Cup.

Ronaldo, the Portuguese captain, scored the only goal in the first game, leading Portugal to a 1–0 victory, but there was still a full ninety-minute game to win in Sweden before Portugal could advance. But while Portugal had played well in the first half, the team had been unable to score a goal in this second game. Several times Ronaldo found himself with the ball in a good position to score, but his shots missed—going either just high or barely wide. And every one of Ronaldo's missed goals gave the home fans more ammunition with which to mock him, hoping their team could capitalize on Portugal's mistakes and get a goal, which they desperately needed.

"I Am Here!"

In the first five minutes of the second half, Portugal was able to draw first blood as Ronaldo received a perfect pass from a teammate and smashed the ball past the goalkeeper, giving Portugal a 1–0 lead in the game. But Sweden would not give up so easily, and it would be the team's 6-foot-5-inch (1.9m) captain and star player, Zlatan Ibrahimovic, who would eventually head in a goal from a corner kick. The home crowd quickly rediscovered their voices and urged their team on for another. Just four minutes later, Ibrahimovic struck a free kick through a wall of Portuguese players and into the back of the net, giving Sweden a 2–1 lead.

It seemed as though all the momentum was now with Sweden. However, the Portuguese players continued fighting, and within five minutes of Ibrahimovic's second goal, Ronaldo sprinted up the field, latched on to a pass, and dribbled with defenders at his heels before shooting it past the Swedish goalkeeper into the net. Having tied up the game, Ronaldo celebrated by racing to the sidelines, looking at the home crowd, and pointing at himself and then the ground. He screamed, "I am here!"[1]

Though the Swedish fans booed lustily, the TV commentators went wild over Ronaldo's impact on the game. "There's one

Cristiano Ronaldo celebrates after scoring the winning goal in the FIFA 2014 World Cup qualifier match between Portugal and Sweden on November 15, 2013.

player on the pitch out there that can turn the course of a game, change the complexion of the match, and it's Cristiano Ronaldo,"[2] said an announcer for Sky Sports, the network covering the match. Portugal had tied the game at 2–2, but Sweden was barely given any time to respond, as Ronaldo once again was on a breakaway—flying past the goalkeeper and firing a shot into the goal, breaking the hearts of the home crowd. Ronaldo had scored a hat trick—three goals in a single game—and sent his team through to the World Cup finals in Brazil. One sports analyst, noting that there seemed to be nothing that Ronaldo could not do for his team, said, laughing, "If it was needed, he'd fly the plane [to Brazil]!"[3]

"He's absolutely incredible," another announcer marveled. "His movement, his first touch, and his finishing tonight [have] just been extraordinary . . . this is why Ronaldo is so renowned in world football [soccer]. Everything about his game is top-notch, and tonight he's just shown why he is the very, very best in the world."[4]

Soccer aficionados throughout the world agreed that Ronaldo played one of the best games of his career that night—certainly the most dramatic. With his leading-man good looks, his incredible skill on the soccer field, and his effusive, contagious excitement in playing the game, Cristiano Ronaldo continues to excite soccer fans throughout the world.

Watching him play, it is hard to imagine that Ronaldo was not a privileged child from a soccer background with opportunities to train at expensive soccer camps or have private lessons. He was, in fact, a boy from a poor neighborhood with humble beginnings. So what path led a skinny kid playing in the streets on an island off the coast of Portugal to become not only one of the world's highest-paid athletes but also one who is considered by many to be the best soccer player on the planet?

Chapter 1

An Island Childhood

With a population of more than 110,000, the city of Funchal, on the island of Madeira off the coast of Portugal, got its name centuries ago from the spice known as *funcho*, called "fennel" in English—one of the most sought-after spices by merchants, and which today is mass-produced on the island. But Funchal today is well known for more than spices. It is famous for its beautiful beaches, the turquoise water surrounding the island, the luxurious hotels, and the exciting nightlife enjoyed by Funchal's many tourists. But in the last decade, Funchal has had an even larger claim to fame—its most well-known native son, Cristiano Ronaldo, is arguably the best soccer player in the world.

A Crowded House

Cristiano Ronaldo, whose full name is Cristiano Ronaldo dos Santos Aveiro, was born on Tuesday, February 5, 1985, in the Santo Antonio neighborhood of Funchal, the capital of Madeira. He was the fourth child of Maria Dolores dos Santos Aveiro and her husband, Jose Dinis Aveiro—known to his friends as Dinis. Ronaldo has an older brother, Hugo, and two sisters, Liliana Catia and Elma.

His parents decided to give him the second name of Ronaldo, after Ronald Reagan, the president of the United States at the time of Ronaldo's birth. The significance of the name "Ronaldo" had nothing at all to do with Reagan's politics but rather had to do with the fact that Ronaldo's father considered Reagan his all-time favorite actor—especially because of Reagan's roles in American cowboy films before he became a politician.

Ronaldo's father was employed as a gardener for the district, and his mother—known as Dolores—worked as both a cook and a housecleaner. Though geographically the family home was not far from the tourist areas of Funchal, it was worlds apart

Funchal—Cristiano Ronaldo's hometown—is the largest city and capital of the Portuguese island of Madeira in the north Atlantic Ocean.

from the posh tourist areas near the sea. Like most of the other houses in the area, Ronaldo's home was tin-roofed, quite small, and for a family of six, very cramped. Ronaldo and his three siblings shared one small bedroom, and his parents had the other. In fact, according to biographer Tom Olds, the family home at one point became so crowded that Ronaldo's father moved the washing machine up to the roof.

Another drawback of the little house was that its walls and roof were exceptionally leaky in wet weather—a serious concern in Madeira because of its frequent rainy days. Ronaldo's mother was adamant that the family home would be cozy, warm, and dry, and so she was always on the lookout for bricks and mortar to bring home so they could mend the leaks. Ronaldo remembers that even though the family was poor, his parents worked extremely hard to keep their children safe and comfortable.

An Island Childhood   **13**

Discovering *Futebol*

As a little boy, Ronaldo was skinny and full of energy, and his family was hopeful that he had a future as an athlete. Dinis, especially, was yearning for a soccer player in the family, for it was his favorite game to watch. Ronaldo's parents knew that his constant need to be active would likely be a detriment to him in most professions. Like many little boys in his neighborhood, he loved playing *futebol* (known as soccer in the United States) every chance he got.

According to Fernao Sousa, Ronaldo's godfather, by the time the boy was two or three years old, he was playing with his beat-

Residents walk at the site where Cristiano Ronaldo was born at Bairro Quinta Falcao, in Funchal, Madeira.

A Sign of Things to Come?

One of the early photos in Ronaldo's baby book shows him in a blue-and-white outfit, wearing white booties. He has gold bracelets on each wrist and a long chain with a gold crucifix. While little Cristiano looks peaceful and happy in the photo, the occasion of that baptismal ceremony was anything but relaxed.

The story of Ronaldo's baptism is a fitting one for a soccer star. His parents scheduled the ceremony soon after his birth, but his father's love of soccer almost derailed the occasion. Besides being the gardener for the town hall in Funchal, Dinis also helped out as equipment manager for the local amateur soccer club, CF Andorinho. Dinis had asked the team captain, Fernao Barros Sousa, to be godfather to his son.

The baptism was scheduled for 6 PM in the church, but Andorinho had an important soccer match that afternoon against its biggest rival, and the game was running late. The priest was nervously pacing in the church because another baptism was scheduled after Ronaldo's. Finally, at 6:30, Dinis and Sousa—happy that their team had won—ran into the church and the ceremony could finally begin.

up football (soccer ball) constantly. In fact, Sousa chuckles as he remembers trying to get little Ronaldo to play with other toys—without success. "One Christmas I gave him a remote-controlled car, thinking that would keep him busy," says Sousa, "but he preferred to play with a football. He slept with his ball, it never left his side. It was always under his arm—wherever he went, it went with him."[5]

Because it was a very poor area, Santo Antonio had no public parks, soccer fields, or organized leagues for children to play in. Ronaldo remembers that beginning at around age five or six, he and his friends usually played in the street, as there were no other playing areas that were available to them:

> I used to play in the street, or, rather, in the Quinta do Falcao road, where I was born, since there was not a sport field in the neighborhood. Me—I was then five or six years old—and my friends would use two stones to mark the width of the goal and we played right there, in the middle of the street, even though it had a steep slope. Because this was a road, we always had to watch out for the traffic. Whenever a bus came along, it had to stop a little while, wait for us to take the "goals" out of the way. . . . Then we started again: replace the stones, remove the stones. And it went on like this.[6]

Watching Out for Mr. Agostinho

Buses were not the only worries for children playing soccer in Ronaldo's neighborhood. Ronaldo recalls how some of the neighbors would complain to his parents that Ronaldo and his soccer pals would kick the ball into their gardens. More than a few of those neighbors vowed that they would keep any ball that came into their yards, and sometimes, he says, those neighbors would keep that promise, and he would run home sobbing over the loss of his precious football.

The most fearsome of the boys' neighbors, Mr. Agostinho, was an avid and very successful gardener. He would become enraged when the boys' footballs landed in his garden, crushing some of his prized flowers. One day he warned the boys that from that time on he would puncture any balls that landed on any of his plants. However, Ronaldo recalls that he did not take Mr. Agostinho's warnings seriously:

> I didn't take any notice because all I wanted to do was play. I took chances and . . . inevitably the ball would land in his garden. Every time that happened, I would run as fast as I could to get the ball out of there. He would complain to my mother, who in turn would tell me off. But the following

day the very same thing would happen again. There was nothing he could do.[7]

Soccer vs. School

Perhaps not surprisingly, Ronaldo's love of soccer began to interfere with school. He was far more interested in more active pursuits, such as soccer, than he was in reading and learning arithmetic. One of his teachers, Maria dos Santos, recalls him as "well behaved, fun, and a good friend to his classmates" but adds that there was no question about his favorite pastime:

> From the day he walked through the door, football was his favorite sport. He took part in other activities, learnt songs and did his work, but he liked to have time for himself, time for football. If there wasn't a real ball around—and often there wasn't—he would make one out of socks. He

A photo shows Cristiano Ronaldo's ID card from the Funchal futebol club for the 1994–1995 season.

An Island Childhood **17**

would always find a way of . . . playing football in the playground. I don't know how he managed it.[8]

His fifth-grade teacher was less patient about her student's preference for *futebol* over school. She scolded him for being chronically late, dashing in the door with his ever-present ball in one hand. "Ronaldo, forget the ball," she would say over and over again. "The ball will not feed you. Do not miss classes. School is what really matters to you, not the ball, that will not bring you anything in life."[9]

Even though Ronaldo did not believe her at the time, he understands today that she was doing her job the correct way.

> Life is full of surprises. At the time I would listen to her without paying much attention. But today I understand her. . . . I still think she did the right thing and that she must keep on following her belief. . . . It was a good piece of advice, as we never know what tomorrow may bring. But I never paid much attention to her.[10]

The Lure of Soccer

He was not a bad student. In fact, he thoroughly enjoyed science class—perhaps because of the island on which he was raised. "Madeira, my island, is volcanic and has a wide variety of plants that turn it into a magnificent garden," he says, looking back on his school days. "These [science] classes attracted my interest, and all my attention was focused on them. . . . I am sorry I did not study more, but I had to make a choice in my life."[11]

The lure of playing soccer was too strong for Ronaldo to resist. He would be on the way to school and just before getting there, would decide to go practice soccer instead. Even when friends did not join him in his skipping school, he found ways to work on skills by himself. There was a well near his house with a large wall—about 215 square feet (20 sq. m) that was perfect for kicking a soccer ball against. Because the ball came back very quickly from the cement wall, it taught him to quicken his reflexes so he could retrieve and control the ball, just as he would

No More "Little Bee"

When Ronaldo was a very young soccer player, he was called "Abelhinha" (Little Bee) because he was small and dribbled the ball quickly with little zig-zag steps. But the nickname grew tiresome for him, because his teammates began to grow while he stayed smaller and skinnier than they were. Even some of his coaches—who were impressed with his foot skills—mentioned that his skinny, short build was a bit of a drawback when playing with taller, stronger players.

Ronaldo knew that the coaches were right, and he devised a plan. He decided to begin eating more at every meal, hoping that the new regimen would help him grow faster. He asked his mother if it he could eat two bowls of soup for each meal, instead of just one. She agreed that it might work, and while nothing happened right away, he gradually began noticing that he was getting a bit taller than he had been. Within two years, he had grown several inches. Even his teammates noticed that he was getting taller.

By the age of seventeen, when he started playing with Sporting Lisbon's first team in 2002, Ronaldo was 5 feet 10 inches (1.5 m)—a height he had never imagined he could reach. Though no one could call him his old nickname, "Abelhinha," he was just as fast with the ball as he had been before.

have to do against a skilled opponent in a game. Each day, as he played on his own or with his friends, his skills were getting sharper, and his determination to play the game was growing stronger.

Like his teachers, Ronaldo's mother also was frustrated by the boy's one-track mind. She was determined that he would get a good education, so when Ronaldo came home from school, she would firmly tell him to go to his room and complete his homework for the next day. "He always told me he didn't have

An Island Childhood

any," she says. "So I would go and start [cooking dinner] and he would chance his luck. He would climb out the window, grab a yogurt or some fruit, and run away with the ball under his arm. He'd be out playing until 9:30 at night."[12]

Tacit Approval

Though Ronaldo's parents wanted him to attend school and do well at his studies, they were torn as to what to do with their son. On the one hand, they realized that he was basically unin-

Dolores Aveiro, Ronaldo's mother, gives a thumbs-up during an event in 2014. When he was growing up, Ronaldo's parents allowed him to focus on athletics at the expense of his school studies.

terested in most of his studies; on the other, he appeared to have the ability to become a fine soccer player who could most likely make a living playing for a professional team someday. For that reason, it is not surprising that they did not force Ronaldo to stay in school. Though his teachers urged Ronaldo's parents to punish him for neglecting his studies, his mother says that she never did, since her son had to practice as much as possible if he was to become a football star.

"It is difficult for many people to understand this quandary that parents face, especially in the poorest and most crime-ridden neighborhoods," says social worker Roberto Navarro, who is very familiar with neighborhoods in Portugal like the one where Ronaldo grew up:

> It's a completely different mindset for parents that are raising children in these dead-end neighborhoods. Like parents everywhere, they want their children to do well in life, to get a better education than they had. But if they have a child that is gifted at football or basketball or some other sport, or can sing like an angel, or has some other amazing talent, the parents begin to think realistically. They say, "Here is our son who is destined to be a great athlete or a famous recording star, and will likely become rich doing so. Why on earth would we insist that he go to school, which he utterly dislikes?"[13]

Years later, Ronaldo suddenly found himself very regretful about spending so little time on his studies back in Madeira—especially his English classes. He says that he realized his mistake the moment he arrived in Manchester, England, as a teenager to join the Manchester United team.

When the team's manager, Alex Ferguson, introduced Ronaldo to his new teammates—including the great Dutch player Ruud van Nistelrooy, whom Ronaldo had idolized—he realized he had made a big mistake years ago in Funchal. Van Nistelrooy smiled pleasantly and said, "How are you?"[14] in English. But as Ronaldo recalls what is still a painful memory, he confesses that he had no idea what van Nistelrooy had said to him. "I stood there, looking at him without knowing what to answer, as I could not understand a word he was saying. Then I remembered all the English classes I had skipped. I needed English after all."[15]

The Best Part of Practicing

When Ronaldo was six years old, his cousin Nuno invited him to come to one of his games. Nuno played on a local team that was part of a large football (soccer) club called Andorinha. He thought that since Ronaldo enjoyed playing *futebol*, he might enjoy coming along sometime and practicing with the team. Thrilled at the suggestion, Ronaldo eagerly began working out with Nuno's team. It was even more fun because Dinis, his father, was the team manager—in charge of the uniforms and balls, and other equipment the boys used for practicing. Ronaldo and his father enjoyed spending time together, and Dinis was extremely proud as he watched his young son shine on the field.

But while Ronaldo thoroughly enjoyed the Andorinha training sessions, many soccer experts say it was actually Ronaldo's daily informal games, known as "kickabouts," with his neighborhood friends that helped him hone his ball-handling skills. Most of the boys he played with were older and stronger than he, and had more experience on the football pitch. To hold his own against them, he had to rely on developing quick feet and agility. Also, the hours spent kicking the ball against the wall was critical, for it helped Ronaldo learn to control the ball with either foot—something that many players are not comfortable with. Many experts believe that it was this solitary work—together with the informal "kickabouts"—that made Ronaldo the creative and highly skilled player he would become.

"The Crybaby" and the "Little Bee"

But Ronaldo was thrilled to train and play real games with the Andorinha team, too. He was lucky enough to have twenty-five-year veteran Francisco Afonso, a skilled and patient man, as his first coach. Though it was clear that Ronaldo was highly skilled in terms of agility and ball control, he had not yet learned the strategic aspects of the game that would be important too.

As Afonso continued to work with the young player, it was clear to the coach that Ronaldo was head and shoulders ahead of his teammates. Afonso still vividly recalls the first time he saw seven-year-old Ronaldo on the field.

> Football was what Cristiano lived for. He was fast, he was technically brilliant and he played equally well with his left and right foot. He was skinny but he was a head taller than other kids his age. He was undoubtedly extremely gifted. . . . He was always chasing the ball, he wanted to be the one to finish the game. . . . And whenever he couldn't play or he missed a game, he was devastated.[16]

It was this need-to-win attitude in Ronaldo that made him the determined player he was, but also made winning far more important to him than it was to most of his teammates. In fact, he gained the nickname "crybaby" because of his emotional reactions to losing. "He cried and got angry very easily—if a teammate didn't pass him the ball, if he or someone else missed a goal or a pass, or if the team wasn't playing how he wanted,"[17] his mother recalls.

Andorinha president Rui Santos vividly remembers a match during the 1993–1994 season, when Ronaldo was eight years old. His team was playing one of the best teams on the island of Madeira, but by halftime, Andorinha was losing 2–0. "Ronaldo was so distraught that he was sobbing like a child who had his favorite toy confiscated," Santos remembers. He says that in this case, Ronaldo's emotional reaction created a spark that resulted in a quick comeback. "In the second half he came onto the pitch and scored two goals, leading the team to a 3–2 victory. He definitely did not like to lose. He wanted to win every time and when they lost, he cried."[18]

Ronaldo also gained another, more positive nickname during his early years playing soccer with Andorinha. Because of his quick feet and his skill in dribbling the ball, he was known as "Abelhinha," or "Little Bee," because no one could catch him on the field. He was proud of that nickname, and years later when

An Island Childhood

A life-size statue of Ronaldo was erected in 2014 in his hometown of Funchal, where twenty years earlier he began to attract attention from professional scouts.

he was living in Madrid, he bought a dog—a Yorkshire Terrier—that he named Abelhinha.

Attracting Attention

By the time he was ten years old, Ronaldo was attracting the attention of scouts for Madeira's most skilled, elite teams. In many European countries, where soccer is by far the most-played and most-watched sport, professional teams keep their eyes open for young phenoms—even children as young as Ronaldo. Their goal is to sign highly promising players before any other team can. In Ronaldo's case, scouts from the two big soccer clubs on the island, Nacional da Madeira and Maritimo, were both very interested in him.

Coincidentally, Rauel Sousa—Ronaldo's godfather—was coaching one of the younger Nacional teams and was floored when he heard some of the team's scouts raving about the young sensation they wanted to sign:

I was delighted to discover that they were talking about my godson. I knew he was playing football, but I had no idea he was so good. He was streets ahead of the rest. He handled the ball beautifully and he definitely had a bright future ahead of him. I immediately realized that this kid could be a godsend [financially] to his family.[19]

After presenting a contract to Ronaldo's parents, Nacional reached an agreement with them, but it was not at all easy. First, Maritimo—the other big team on the island—was Ronaldo's favorite team. Notes biographer Luca Caioli, "His heart beats for Maritimo."[20] Also, Dinis, Ronaldo's father, was hoping that his son would sign with Maritimo because the team's home field was very close to the family's house; that would make it easier and cheaper for his parents and siblings to watch all of his matches.

A meeting was scheduled with both teams, so Ronaldo's parents could make a decision on which was the better choice for their son. However, when the Maritimo representative missed the meeting, Dinis and Dolores decided that their son would sign a contract with Nacional. Without realizing it, the ten-year-old had just made his first step toward a professional career.

Chapter 2

Club Soccer

Barely ten years old when he arrived at the Nacional training facility, Cristiano Ronaldo was virtually trembling with excitement, anxious to start training. His mother, however, was more concerned than excited. She was very worried that her son would get hurt. "My husband was always encouraging him to play with older kids," she remembers. "I was worried he could hurt himself or break a leg, but Dinis always said, 'Don't worry, they can't catch him, he's too fast.'"[21]

But this was the first time Ronaldo would be playing with players as skilled and talented as he, and it seemed that all of them were far bigger and stronger than he was. The trainers at Nacional noticed how skinny he was, too, and immediately wanted him to start eating more to fill out his gangly frame.

Evaluating the New Player

Though Ronaldo's coaches and trainers had concerns about the skinny ten-year-old's weight, they were highly impressed with his abilities on the field. Antonio Mendoca, who coached Ronaldo for the first two seasons at Nacional, recalls, "His skills were already highly developed: speed, dribbling, shooting, lightning execution. Street football had taught him how to avoid getting hit, sidestep the opponent and face up to kids much bigger than he was. It had also strengthened his character—he was extremely courageous."[22]

The Estádio da Madeira (Madeira Stadium), seen in a photo from 2009, is the home base for the Nacional da Madeira—the team where Ronaldo started his professional career.

However, there was one aspect of his game that did need improvement, and that was for Ronaldo to remember that soccer was a team sport. Since he began playing, he had always relied on his ability to dribble the ball down the field himself and to score almost at will—virtually a team unto himself. But Nacional's teams stressed cooperation on the field—something Ronaldo was not used to.

Besides being unaccustomed to relying on teammates, Ronaldo did not like to be corrected by his coaches—especially in front of the other boys. When his teammates made mistakes and things did not go Nacional's way during a game, Ronaldo would get angry and cry. If he had been only a mediocre player, the other boys on his team would likely have mocked him mercilessly, but Mendoca says that there was a big reason why they tolerated his emotional outbursts. "[His teammates] put up with it because he used to score so many goals," says Mendoca. "We won all our games nine– or ten–nil [zero]."[23]

Scheduling a Tryout

Though it was assumed that Ronaldo would be at Nacional for several years developing his game, it was not long before some of the larger Portuguese teams on the mainland began taking an interest in him. They were highly impressed—especially after he helped Nacional win the regional league title for the ten-to-twelve-year-old division.

It was Fernao Sousa, Ronaldo's godfather, who decided it would be best to let other coaches see firsthand how talented the boy was. In March 1997, Sousa contacted Joao Marques Freitas, a high-ranking official of Sporting Lisbon (often just referred to as "Sporting"), a well-established athletic association in Portugal that is renowned throughout Europe for its talented youth soccer teams. In fact, many of Europe's most famous soccer players have been products of Sporting Lisbon.

Sousa wanted Freitas to watch Ronaldo play to see if he thought the boy had a future playing professionally. Freitas agreed to evaluate Ronaldo, and after watching him in action during a game, he excitedly called Sporting Lisbon and urged the association to schedule a tryout for Ronaldo as soon as possible. Within days, Sousa was driving his godson to the airport. The eleven-year-old traveled by himself—the first time he had ever been on an airplane. With his identification card around his neck, he blinked back tears as he waved goodbye to his family.

Ronaldo's tryout for Sporting Lisbon was overseen by coaches Paulo Cardoso and Osvaldo Silva. Their first reaction upon seeing the boy was similar to that of Nacional's coaches—that he seemed too small and scrawny. And Ronaldo's anxiety almost ruined his first training session. "I was about to control the first pass they made to me," he remembers, "and the ball slipped from under my foot, but I thought, 'Take it easy, you can do it.'"[24]

He was absolutely right. Once Ronaldo began to play, the coaches were impressed. They watched him easily steal a pass from an older player and dribble it up the field, even while being pursued by three highly skilled opponents. Though the newcomer was small and skinny, there was no question that Ronaldo would be a welcome addition at Sporting.

Saved by the Desire to Win

In his biography of Cristiano Ronaldo, Tom Oldfield notes that while his time at Sporting Lisbon was at first difficult for the youngster, it was his competitive spirit—his hatred of losing—that gave him the strength to stay in a place that was so far from home.

> He would not let any obstacle block his path. Having overcome the homesickness, there was a sense that he had beaten the most challenging opponent and that stardom and the Sporting senior team now beckoned. He was still physically small and very skinny but he had pace and skill—vital commodities for any winger. A former coach remembers not only Ronaldo's will to win but also the effect that he had on his teammates. Ronaldo cried, shouted, and fussed when results did not go his team's way, but this reaction appeared to energize his colleagues, getting a reaction from them and inspiring them to follow his example on the pitch.
>
> Cristiano's competitive nature is also confirmed by Portuguese international goalkeeper Ricardo. In his book *Diary of a Dream*, "Whether it is ping-pong, table football, darts or snooker, he does not let up. If there are people who were born for the game and for competition, Cristiano Ronaldo is one of them." . . . A growth spurt had left Cristiano with an awkward physique, not necessarily well suited to a career as a professional footballer, and he had to work hard to strengthen his body. . . . Cristiano knew he had to toughen up if he wanted to win a regular role in the first team and he applied himself to this task as ably as he had to all the other obstacles he had faced in life.

Tom Oldfield. *Cristiano Ronaldo: The £80 Million Man—The Inside Story of the Greatest Footballer on Earth*. London: John Blake, 2009, pp. 15–16.

Signing with Sporting

Cardoso and Silva immediately recommended to Sporting's director, Aurelio Pereira, that he come to the next day's practice and see the youngster for himself. If Pereira had any doubts about Ronaldo's abilities, they were dispelled immediately as he watched him play. As he later recalled:

> He was talented, he could play with both feet, he was incredibly fast and when he played it was as if the ball was an extension of his body. But what impressed me more was his determination. His strength of character shone through. He was courageous—mentally speaking, he was indestructible. And he was fearless, unfazed by older players. He had the kind of leadership qualities that only the greatest players have. One of a kind. When they got back to the dressing room all the other boys were clamoring to talk to him and get to know him. He had it all, and it was clear he would only get better.[25]

Not surprisingly, Pereira was determined to sign Ronaldo immediately. He knew that a boy of his ability level was rare, and it would be far better to have Ronaldo on a Sporting Lisbon team than to have Sporting teams play against him in the league. Within a week, Pereira had offered him a position at Sporting. Interestingly, Pereira was so determined to sign Ronaldo, he bought out Ronaldo's contract with Nacional for the sum of 22,500 euros (approximately 27,300 dollars). Experts say that such a payment was incredibly rare—in fact, it was virtually unheard of for a team to pay anything for such a young player, let alone more than 27,000 dollars.

Ronaldo Moves away from Home

Ronaldo was pleased to have done so well in his tryout and was eager to begin playing with Sporting Lisbon. However, in the last week of August 1997, as the time drew nearer to leave Madeira for the mainland of Portugal, the reality of leaving home was dawning on him. The effect of his moving 600 miles (966km)

Cristiano Ronaldo (right) and a fellow Sporting Lisbon player train in July 2002.

away from home would be profound. Only twelve years old, he would be moving to surroundings totally unfamiliar to him, and for the first time in his life, he would be without the security of his family on which he depended.

The sadness hit hard as his family took him to the airport, Ronaldo remembers, and it got worse at the airport when he finally had to say goodbye. "My sisters and my mother were crying," he says. "I was crying. Even when I was on the plane and we had just taken off, I thought of my family crying about me and I started to cry again."[26]

For the first few weeks after he arrived in Lisbon, things were no better. The city was loud and bustling with traffic and crowds of people on the move—a radical difference from the quiet pace of life in Madeira. He had difficulty getting used to the noise and the swarms of people. Though he was assigned to a dormitory with ten other boys with whom he made friends, he was lonely and missed his family.

"I Felt Like a Clown"

The Sporting Lisbon players were not only expected to dedicate themselves to learning the skills and strategies of soccer. They were also expected to continue their education at the nearby Cristfal Day School. Sporting Lisbon demanded that the players conduct themselves appropriately and give their schoolwork the same close attention that they were giving to soccer.

However, Ronaldo's first day of school was a disaster. By the time he found his way to his classroom, he was quite late; the teacher was already taking attendance. One at a time, the pupils were asked to introduce themselves. When it was his turn, Ronaldo said his name and began to tell them that he had come from Madeira, when he heard some of the other students laughing at him. His island accent was quite different from the Portuguese commonly spoken in Lisbon, and his classmates were mocking him.

"To me, it was very strange to find that no one understood what I said," Ronaldo remembers. "There were times when I thought I spoke a different language from my colleagues and I found that very confusing. As soon as I opened my mouth, they immediately started laughing and mocking. I was traumatized. I felt like a clown. I cried with shame."[27]

A New Nickname

Like the other boys that had come to Sporting from a long distance away, Ronaldo had purchased a prepaid telephone card so he could call home when he needed to speak to his family. It was soothing to hear his parents' and siblings' voices, and it helped to tell them about the difficulties he was having:

I called my mother saying that I could not stand it anymore, that the other kids were making fun of me, that I wanted to return home. "Go on, do not pay attention to what the others say," my mother and the rest of my family would say. They always gave me the will to continue. I did not give up, thanks to them. Eventually I became used to those episodes and my colleagues also began to get tired, and to understand that it was not right to do all that mocking.[28]

Cristiano Ronaldo lies injured in 2002 during his time playing for Sporting Lisbon. When he started playing in Lisbon, Ronaldo was so sad and homesick that his teammates would call him a crybaby.

A Ferrari or a Garbage Can?

In their book, *CR7: The Secrets of the Machine,* authors Luis Miguel Pereira and Juan Ignacio Gallardo tell of Ronaldo's frequent infractions of the rules at Sporting Lisbon. The Sporting manager at the time, Nuno Nare, was concerned about how homesick Ronaldo and some of the other boys were. They lived too far away to go home on weekends, so it was not surprising that they were often sad, and maybe that was one of the reasons Ronaldo acted out. Nare decided to find ways to make life on the weekends more fun. Luckily for Ronaldo, sometimes even the punishments for misbehavior became fun.

> One of the penalties for breaking the internal rules was to empty those big trash cans with wheels. Ronaldo emptied quite a few, in exchange for the same number of school violations. While his mates watched TV in the common room, the Madeiran (Cristiano) would go by with the trash can and hear their provocations: "Vrommmm! Vrommmm!"
>
> "They were so capable of transforming a punishment into fun that they even called the trash can the Ferrari," reveals Nuno Nare. "Go and empty the Ferrari," his colleagues would shout, and Cristiano would predict, "One day I'm going to have one." And he did, not one but several. A true family was created. "We performed miracles," concludes Nuno Nare.

Luis Miguel Pereira and Juan Ignacio Gallardo. *CR7: Secrets of the Machine.* Estoril, Portugal: Prime, 2014 (e-book), chapter 2.

But while talking with his family relieved some of the stress he was feeling, the frequent calls were actually making him even sadder. He would race to the phone whenever he needed to talk, but hanging up after a conversation, he found himself lonelier than before, and he would cry. Ronaldo began re-evaluating his decision to join Sporting Lisbon. He was so visibly unhappy, in fact, that the other boys gave him the nickname "Xora," the Portuguese word meaning "to cry."

His coaches and teachers were becoming aware of the grief and anxiety Ronaldo was experiencing—in fact, it was not the first time they had seen island boys who had a great deal of difficulty adjusting to life at Sporting Lisbon, according to one of Sporting Lisbon's recruiters, Aurelio Pereira. "I saw that players who came from Madeira, at 15 or 16, had their bag packed again on the second day and were ready to leave, because they missed their family so much; they had that melancholy that is typical of the islands."[29]

But something had to be done to keep their most promising young recruit from returning home. They knew that Ronaldo's mother had a great deal of influence on him, and quickly made arrangements to fly her from Madeira to Lisbon to visit. Her visits buoyed his spirits considerably, and eventually led to him becoming far more comfortable at Sporting.

The Consequences of Misbehaving

But while he was gradually getting used to his new surroundings, he and his fellow soccer players had to learn that there are consequences for any misbehavior, whether in the classroom or on the soccer field. Ronaldo learned this the hard way. He had been misbehaving at school—in one case, actually threatening one of his teachers with a chair because Ronaldo believed the man had disrespected him. Days later, he talked back to a coach who asked him to clean up the changing room. According to biographer Luca Caioli, Ronaldo refused, announcing to the coach, "I'm a Sporting player, and I don't have to pick up anything off the floor."[30]

Not surprisingly, these incidents did not sit well with the team's directors. Though they were aware of Ronaldo's talent and future importance to Sporting Lisbon, they decided to punish him in a way that would teach him a lesson. Ronaldo's Sporting team had recently made it to the playoffs, and he was very excited about the coming games. He had become even more excited when he learned that his team was going to play Maritimo, one of the teams on his home island of Madeira. Not surprisingly, Ronaldo was counting the days until that match. He could not wait to return to Madeira and play in front of his family and friends in the famous green and white uniform of Sporting.

But Sporting's directors decided that as a consequence of his misbehavior, they would not allow Ronaldo to go to Madeira. Many years later, Ronaldo still remembers how he felt the moment he checked the list of players scheduled to make the trip. "I saw the list and I wasn't on it," he says. "I checked it four times and . . . nothing. I started crying and stormed into the training centre, angrily demanding an explanation. It was tough but I learned a very important lesson."[31]

A Heart Scare

Ronaldo was upset to have been left out of the trip to Madeira, but he was glad when the team returned and he resumed playing. The Sporting coaches continued to be pleased with his progress and were confident that as long as he could avoid injuries, he was going to be a star player.

However, when Ronaldo was fifteen, he began noticing that his heart would sometimes start racing for no apparent reason. Even when he was sitting down, his heart would occasionally beat as fast as it would if he were running at top speed. Besides beating far faster than normal, his heart rhythm was also irregular. But at the time no one gave it much thought, since after his physical exam at the start of the season team doctors had classified his heart as being fit for playing.

But doctors became worried when Ronaldo began mentioning that his heart was pounding. He also confided to one of the Sporting Lisbon staff that he got tired very easily. When the medical staff began monitoring his pulse, they became worried about the possibility that Ronaldo had a serious heart ailment—even one that could end his football career. In fact, noted Luis Miguel Pereira and Juan Ignacio Gallardo in their book *CR7: The Secrets of the Machine*, "cardiac anomalies are the most frequent cause of sudden death in sportsmen under the age of 35."[32]

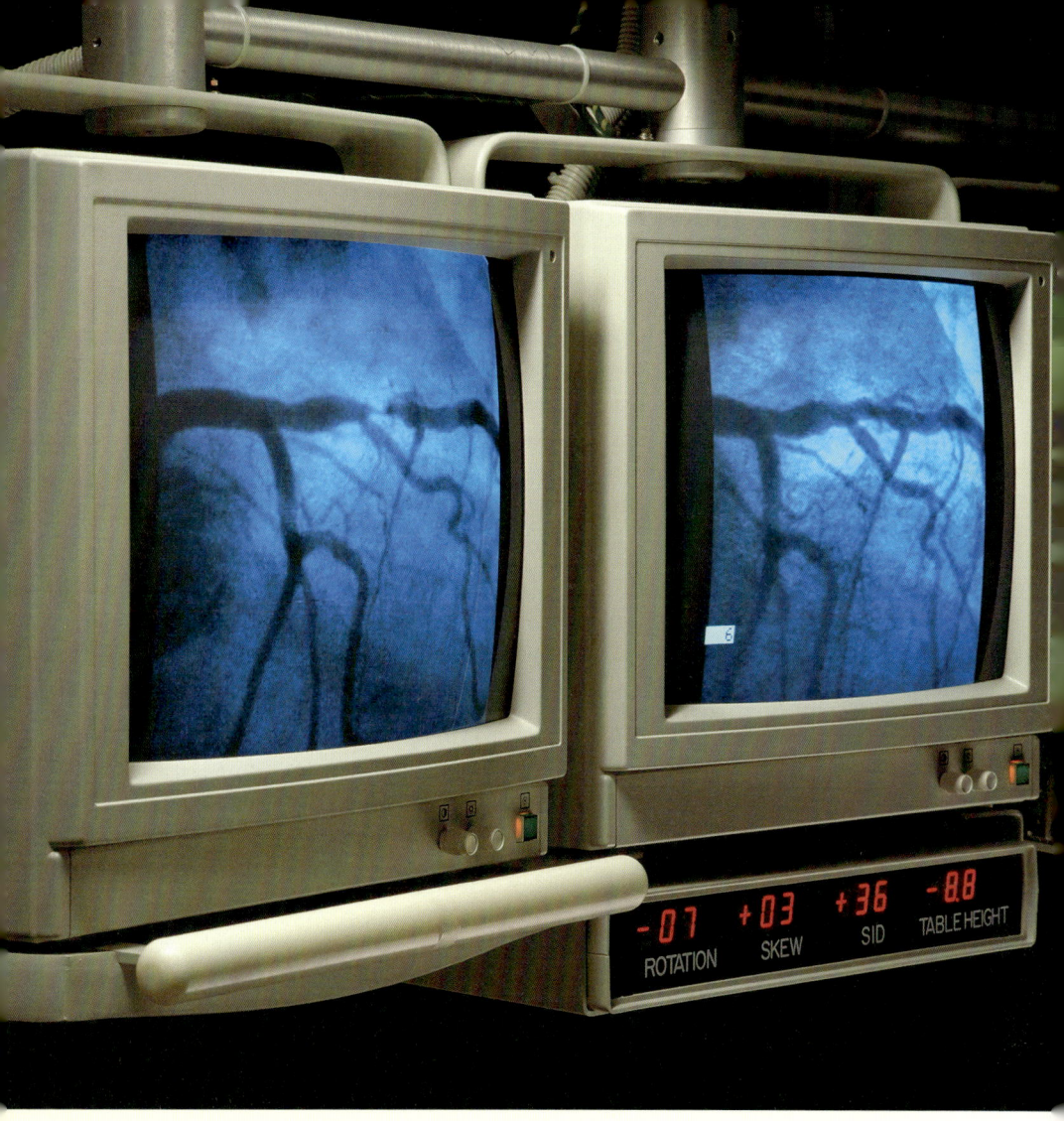

Video monitors display a heart during a cardiac catheterization procedure, the type of operation that saved Cristiano Ronaldo's life.

It seemed clear that the problem would not be solved until doctors could operate on him to determine what was causing his racing and irregular heartbeat. Ronaldo's mother was contacted, and she immediately traveled to the mainland from Madeira so she could sign an authorization that would allow surgeons to operate on her son's heart.

Club Soccer 37

A Relief

The procedure, called a catheter ablation, is neither rare nor terribly difficult. As cardiologist William Scott, co-director of the Children's Medical Center in Dallas, Texas, explains, the procedure used on Ronaldo and other young people with similar conditions is quite common and very effective:

> [It's] a minimally invasive heart procedure where small wires are placed in the large veins of the leg and advance to the heart. These wires are used to make an electrical "map" of the heart that identifies the cause of the abnormal heart rate. Once identified, the problem can be eliminated by heating the small area of the heart involved using a special catheter [flexible tube]. The heat destroys the abnormal tissue and cures the condition.[33]

As it turned out, Ronaldo's heart problem was much less serious than the doctors and coaches had feared, so the heated tube was able to get rid of the problem. As Dolores recalls, "He was operated on in the morning and came out at the end of the afternoon. Before we knew exactly what he had, I was worried, because there was the possibility of him giving up playing football. But the treatment went well, and after some days he was back at training again."[34]

Improving Every Day

With his heart ailment corrected, Ronaldo quickly began to move up the ranks of Sporting Lisbon. In fact, at the age of fifteen, he became the only Sporting player ever to play on the under-16s, under-17s, under-18s, the second team, and the first team in one season. He was tremendously excited at age sixteen when his coach told him that he would have a chance to play in a game with the first team—the elite squad of Sporting.

This was a huge opportunity, for most of the players were five or six years older than he was. Their games were well attended by fans, and he was thrilled just to have a chance to suit up with them, to wear the uniform only the first team could

Sporting Lisbon team members—including a young Cristiano Ronaldo (with the ball)—participate in a training session in June 2004.

Club Soccer **39**

wear. Though he knew it would be a while before he would be a steady member of that first team, he was excited to have the experience of taking the field—even for a few minutes of the game—with the elite players of Sporting he idolized.

During this time, Ronaldo was taking more and more interest in improving his strength and endurance. Even though the players trained for hours every day, he wanted to do even more. There was a gym next to the training facility that had weights and other equipment, and he spent many solitary hours there, usually without permission. During one holiday when he returned to Madeira, he devised a way to build up his leg muscles—he would run long distances with heavy sand bags tied to his legs. The extra weight forced his legs to work harder and, as a result, increased both his strength and his endurance.

Worries from Home

At the same time that Ronaldo was finding success by working hard to improve his fitness and skills as a player, he was distracted by news from home. His brother, Hugo, who had begun using illegal drugs at the age of fourteen, had been in treatment, which Dolores had paid for with her wages as a cleaning worker. But Hugo had had a relapse and required another stay in the treatment facility—and the family did not have the money. Ronaldo was glad to send his monthly check to his mother to use for Hugo's treatment.

However, there was more distressing news. His father, who had battled alcoholism most of his adult life, was having difficulties, too. Ronaldo was close to his father, and this news was heartbreaking. Dinis had always been Ronaldo's biggest fan when his son was younger, attending every game, and cheering enthusiastically from the sidelines. Since Ronaldo had begun playing at Sporting, Dinis eagerly pored over the newspaper to find his son's name in the results of the game the day before—and bragged to all of his friends about Ronaldo's accomplishments.

While Ronaldo was sad and worried about his father's struggles with alcohol and his brother's substance abuse problems,

Ronaldo was also feeling a sense of pride and excitement over improving as a player at Sporting Lisbon. Though he did not know it, his time at Sporting Lisbon would soon come to a close. Very soon, he would be moving on to greater things.

Chapter 3

The Most Expensive Teenager in Britain

Ronaldo's coaches were happy with his progress at Sporting. They were pleased by the strength and weight work he was doing and also noticed that he was becoming faster and smarter as a player. When he was seventeen, he was told to begin training regularly with Sporting's first team—the professional squad.

But while his coaches were impressed with his skills on the field, at first they were limiting his playing time—usually not more than fifteen or twenty minutes at a time. At first that was fine with Ronaldo, for he was in awe of the other players. He desperately wanted to play, but at the same time was fearful of making a mistake that would land him back on a lower team, or even worse, that would lose the game.

An Exciting Goal

But little by little, with each game, his confidence grew, and his teammates became more impressed. In a game against Spain's very talented Seville Real Betis team, Ronaldo was put into the game with only thirteen minutes left to play and the score tied. As regulation time ticked off, the game went into overtime—the next goal for either team would win the match.

Soon into the overtime, a Seville player lost the ball, and before he could react and regain control, Ronaldo stole it and raced toward the left wing, as Luca Caioli reports:

Cristiano is on it like a shot.... He dribbles towards Betis goalie Toni Prats, and from an impossibly tight position on the far left corner of the area, he spies the open goal and aims for the far corner, evading [defender] Rivas, whose desperate leap to deflect it is in vain. It's a phenomenal goal, demonstrating ability, technique, control, potential, and instinct in the box.[35]

Ronaldo's celebration was as memorable as his goal. He ran around on the field, blowing kisses to fans in the stands. It was a moment to remember, he says, but the time when he truly knew he belonged was later that season, when he was chosen to start the game against Sporting's rival Moreirense (another Portuguese team) and scored two beautiful goals. With Sporting's fans cheering and screaming his name, no longer was he nervous and frightened about playing with Sporting's first team.

Attracting International Attention

In the days and weeks following his start with Sporting's professional team, Ronaldo became one of the most-watched soccer players in Europe. It seemed that half of Europe was paying close attention to the exciting teenager from Portugal, and it was not only the spectators. Chelsea, a premier team in England, was very interested. So was the professional Italian team Inter Milan, Real Madrid, and another English premier team, Arsenal. "All seven or eight of the best teams wanted him,"[36] remembers Jorge Mendes, Ronaldo's agent.

Reporters surrounded Ronaldo at an Under-21 Tournament in Toulon, France, and asked him whether, as an eighteen-year-old, he was overwhelmed by all the attention he was getting from clubs eager to sign him. "I don't feel pressured by it all," he insisted:

> I am just excited and happy to know that the big clubs and the top names have noticed me. It gives me strength and encouragement to try to improve every day. But I haven't spoken to anyone yet, and no one has made a concrete

Cristiano Ronaldo (left) of Portugal steals the ball from Marcos Charras of Argentina during the Under-21 Tournament in Toulon, France, in 2003.

offer to Sporting. I know there's a lot of talk in the press, but right now my main objective is to get the [Sporting] team to the final and help them win. That's what I have to focus on.[37]

Two Different Games

There are hundreds of professional soccer leagues around the world, tightly packed with competition to build the best teams and win championships. From the U.S. Major League Soccer (MLS) to the Chinese Super League, to Italy's Serie A, to Brazil's Campeonato Brasileiro Série A, each league boasts some of the most talented players and managers in the world. What makes many of these leagues special, however, is the style that is associated with them.

Italy's top level, the Serie A, has been labeled "defensive" or "Catenaccio football" (literal translation: door-bolt). Arguably two of the top leagues in the world, the English Premier League and the Spanish Primera Division, have very distinct styles that attract and repel certain players. Cristiano Ronaldo is an example of a player who has had the opportunity to not only play in both leagues but also win championships and thrive as a player in both.

The English Premier League is known for playing a very physical and fast-paced game; if a player receives the ball, he expects to be chased or tackled by a defender within seconds. While there is still tough defending in the Spanish league, there is not as much of a rush in possession of the ball; players are allowed to be creative, and defenders are not constantly pressing and rushing at them. Players who are technically gifted at dribbling and play with more finesse do not always succeed in the premier league as they might in the Spanish league. Each league is different and has its own unique characteristics that borrow from cultures around the world. It is a testament to Ronaldo's skill and adaptability that he has been superb in both.

He helped Sporting beat a very talented Italian team to win the tournament. But as throngs of screaming fans turned out at the Lisbon airport to welcome home their team, they were disappointed to see that Ronaldo was not with them. In fact, he was in France, meeting with Sir Alex Ferguson, the coach of the team he would play on next.

The 17.6-Million-Dollar Athlete

One of the teams that had been the most persistent about signing Ronaldo was Manchester United (often referred to simply as MU), coached by legendary Sir Alex Ferguson. An extremely talented coach and judge of talent, he had been following Ronaldo's progress since the boy was fifteen and was highly impressed with him. In 2003, Ferguson wanted to sign the eighteen-year-old before any of the other teams had a chance.

The contract would transfer Ronaldo from Sporting Lisbon to Manchester United for the sum of 15 million euros (the equivalent of 17.6 million dollars). The idea was that Ronaldo would not begin playing for Manchester for some time, but would re-

Sir Alex Ferguson shakes Cristiano Ronaldo's hand after signing him to play for Manchester United in a contract worth 15 million euros.

main for another year or so at Sporting—becoming a more seasoned player—until he was deemed ready to be called up to play with MU. All that remained to be done was for Ronaldo to sign the contract.

The deal would not be made public until after the upcoming *friendly* against Manchester United. (A friendly is a match between two teams that has no importance in the standings of either.) The occasion was special because Sporting had just completed construction of its brand new stadium, and the match with MU would be the facility's first. Not surprisingly, the stands were packed with enthusiastic fans eager not only to see the new stadium but also, more importantly, to cheer on Sporting against the talented Manchester United team.

A Change of Plans

Ronaldo was eager to do well in the match, especially because he wanted to show Ferguson that he was worth the huge sum of money MU was paying Sporting to have him. He was successful in that objective, playing an almost perfect game. He made a beautiful pass to a teammate who in turn scored the first Sporting goal, and continued to impress the crowd with his spectacular dribbling, steals from MU, lightning speed, and even several crowd-pleasing bicycle kicks.

At halftime, Ferguson was having second thoughts about the details of the contract. He told a staffer that he did not want to leave Lisbon without Ronaldo. The Manchester players were feeling the same way during halftime in their locker room. "We were all saying to the boss: 'We've got to sign him,'"[38] recalls MU defender Phil Neville.

So when the match was over, Ronaldo was told that he and his agent, Jorge Mendes, were going to travel to England. He was not surprised; he just assumed that he was going to tour the facilities at Manchester, have a medical evaluation by team doctors, sign the contract, and return to Lisbon to continue training with Sporting until he was called up to play with MU.

Because he did not understand much English, he had no idea what Mendes and the Manchester lawyers were discussing. So when he signed the contract, he was floored when Ferguson told him that they wanted him to remain in Manchester. Shocked, Ronaldo told them that all of his things were back in Lisbon, and that he had not yet said goodbye to his family. Ferguson reassured him: he would train in England, but he could return to Portugal soon to get his belongings.

While he was aware that MU had paid millions of dollars to Sporting Lisbon, Ronaldo was also astonished at the salary he would be paid by his new team. Since being on the first team at Sporting, he had been getting a monthly salary of 2,000 euros per month (2,356 dollars) at Sporting Lisbon—much of it going back to his parents in Madeira. As a Manchester United player, he would start out earning 150,000 euros (176,747 dollars) per month—an astronomical raise!

Ferguson went to great lengths to reassure Ronaldo's family, too—especially his mother, who was concerned about her son going to live so far away. She says that Ferguson promised that he would be sure to keep an eye on Ronaldo in England, since he had no family there. "Ferguson is an exceptional person," Dolores said. "My son has a second father in Manchester who looks after him."[39]

First Impressions

But as word got out about the acquisition of the teenager from Portugal, many Manchester United fans were not sold on the deal. They wondered whether such a young, virtually untested player could be worth that much money. In an article for the English newspaper *The Guardian* on August 13, 2003—just seven days after the contract was signed—reporter Dan Taylor pointed out that Ronaldo, with only twenty-five first-team appearances on Sporting Lisbon, had become "the most expensive teenager in the history of the British game."[40]

Some Manchester United fans were even more concerned about the wisdom of signing Ronaldo when they saw photographs of him at his first public appearance at the Manchester offices. Instead of dressing up for the important occasion, Ronaldo was wearing a see-through white T-shirt and ragged faded

At first, some Manchester United fans were unhappy that Cristiano Ronaldo had been given jersey number seven. Several legendary players for the team, including David Beckham (shown in 2003), had previously worn the number.

The Most Expensive Teenager in Britain 49

blue jeans, and was sporting highlights in his hair. Not surprisingly, some of the older fans were not exactly impressed with his appearance.

But it was the Manchester jersey with the number 7 that brought out some anger among fans. His predecessors who had worn that number included most of MU's greatest players—from George Best and Eric Cantona to the superstar David Beckham, who had recently been traded to Real Madrid. Some fans believed that it was a little premature to assign that special number to a teenage rookie.

Interestingly, Ronaldo had a response to that criticism—one that charmed even the most outspoken critics of the deal:

> The number 7 shirt is an honor and a responsibility. I hope it brings me a lot of luck. Everyone in Manchester has been telling me about Best and Cantona. . . . I'm proud to follow in their footsteps. But there's something that the Brits don't know—number 7 is also special to me because it's the number that Luis Figo wore at Sporting. I have wanted to be like him since I was a little kid, and wear the number 7, just like my great friend Quaresma, who is now wearing it at Barcelona. Both of us can now say that our dreams have come true.[41]

Debut at Old Trafford

Three days later, Ronaldo suited up for his first game in that controversial number 7 jersey when Manchester hosted the Bolton Wanderers for the first game of the season. He was astonished by the size of Old Trafford—MU's stadium; the facility was even more amazing filled with over seventy thousand screaming fans. Not surprisingly, Ronaldo was both confident and awestruck. For the first sixty minutes of the game, he sat on the bench, watching intently as his team struggled to hold on to a 1–0 lead.

With thirty minutes left to play, Ronaldo heard Ferguson call his name, telling him that he was going in. Ronaldo tore off his warm-up suit as quickly as he could, hoping he could make a

Cristiano Ronaldo greets fans during his first match playing for Manchester United at the Old Trafford stadium on August 16, 2003.

good first impression by doing something to help his team win. He remembers:

> The supporters gave me a standing ovation. I was so moved and filled with enthusiasm by that whole atmosphere and the kindness shown on my debut, in short, I did not want to wake up from that wonderful dream. The first time I touched the ball, things went very well. I scored a penalty. The game ended but I wanted it to continue.[42]

The Most Expensive Teenager in Britain

An Unexpected Honor

He had done well—in fact, Ferguson noted afterwards that Ronaldo had played so well that Old Trafford's crowd was on their feet because of the excitement he brought to the game: "It looks like the fans have a new hero," he said. "It was a marvelous debut, almost unbelievable."[43]

However, he cautioned that it was important to give Ronaldo time to get used to the MU system of play, since he was so young. "We have to be careful with the boy. You must remember he is only 18," he warned. "We are going to have to gauge when we use him."[44]

Even more exciting than his coach's kind words, Ronaldo says, was that his new teammates honored him by naming him man of the match. "I was considered the best player on the field," he says, "and I received my first bottle of Champagne, the 'trophy' that is offered in England to the man of the match."[45]

Ronaldo did well during the first season, accumulating eight goals in thirty-nine games—quite impressive for a newcomer. Even more exciting, the MU fans voted him the Sir Matt Busby Player of the Year. That award, named after a famous coach of MU, is determined by fans' votes for their favorite player of the season, and Ronaldo was overwhelmed with gratitude.

Martunis the Survivor

One of the most moving experiences for Ronaldo had nothing whatsoever to do with goals or victories on the soccer field. Instead, it was his opportunity to meet a seven-year-old boy from Indonesia named Martunis, a survivor of one of the most destructive storms in history. Martunis, and his amazing story, would have a lasting effect on Ronaldo and his teammates—something that none of them would ever forget.

Early in 2005, a news story of an event in Southeast Asia was to have a profound effect on Ronaldo and his MU teammates. Less than a month before, on December 26, 2004, a huge underwater earthquake in the Indian Ocean had created a series of violent tsunamis, which left destruction and death in their wake.

Visiting Martunis in Banda Aceh

After the tsunami disaster in Indonesia, and several months after Ronaldo and his Manchester United teammates had brought Martunis and his father to Manchester for a visit, Ronaldo kept his promise to the seven-year-old boy. A few months later Ronaldo made the trip to visit the boy in Banda Aceh—one of the places that suffered the most destruction from the horrific storm.

Martunis was excited to host Ronaldo, and even more excited to receive the gifts the soccer star had brought for him. The best one, he said, was the cell phone Ronaldo gave him. He wanted to try it out, and immediately asked Ronaldo for his phone number. The two sat together, taking turns calling one another. When Ronaldo opened his computer and showed Martunis the computer games he had, the boy was even more thrilled.

Communicating with the help of an interpreter, Ronaldo and Martunis further cemented their friendship. The boy told Ronaldo that his dream was to become a soccer player when he was older. That had always been his dream, he said, but during the time he was trying to stay alive during the tsunami, that was one of the things that kept him from giving up. It is not difficult to understand why Ronaldo was as honored to meet Martunis as the boy was to meet his soccer idol.

More than 230,000 people—most of them in Indonesia—were killed and swept out to sea by the gigantic walls of water.

The story two weeks after the storm was about a seven-year-old boy named Martunis, who had been found on the island of Sumatra. Martunis had been swept out to sea after being separated from his father. Somehow the boy had survived for almost three weeks by drinking sea water and packages of instant noodles and anything else he could find. Finally he was discovered by a reporter on a beach in northern Sumatra. Martunis was dehydrated, covered with insect bites, and near death when he was found. His mother and sisters had been killed, but he was eventually reunited with his father and grandmother.

Seven-year-old tsunami survivor Martunis receives a jersey from Cristiano Ronaldo at an event in Portugal on June 2, 2005.

Moved by the story, Ronaldo wanted to find a way to help Martunis. His idea was to bring the boy over to Manchester and then to Portugal—since Martunis was clearly a fan of Portugal's national team. "We already have people working on this to help make it happen as soon as possible," Ronaldo announced. "I hope we can arrange it, because this boy is a symbol of bravery, and . . . I'm sure he would love to come."[46]

As it turned out, Martunis did visit and was thrilled to spend time with the team—especially with his idol, Cristiano Ronaldo. The team showered him with gifts—his favorite being an actual Portuguese national team jersey, with "Martunis" and the number 1 written on the back. Ronaldo promised to visit him in Indonesia someday soon.

A Death in the Family

The year 2006 was a World Cup year, and no matter which professional teams soccer players were on during the regular league season, a great many went back to their country of origin to play for their native land. As a citizen of Portugal, twenty-one-year-old Ronaldo was eager to play with the Portuguese team. He had been a spectator four years before, when Portugal was eliminated in the third match by the South Korean team. This year, he intended to help his native land win the World Cup.

However, as Ronaldo and his teammates were preparing for the World Cup competition, he received some heart-wrenching news. Dinis, his father, was extremely ill. Having been an alcoholic most of his adult life, Dinis had acute liver and kidney damage—so severe that those organs no longer functioned. The only possible solution, doctors in Funchal's hospital said, was to do a liver transplant.

Ronaldo paid to have his father airlifted from Funchal to a London clinic that specializes in such procedures. While Dinis did improve for a short time, the damage was simply too extensive, and he passed away on September 6, 2005.

Luiz Felipe Scolari, the coach of Portugal's World Cup team, insisted that Ronaldo return to his family and take the time he needed to grieve over his father's death. However, Ronaldo

Cristiano Ronaldo arrives at his father's funeral in Funchal, Madeira, on September 10, 2005.

refused. The next game—against a very strong Russian team—would determine whether Portugal would get into the World Cup. Ronaldo told his coach that he wanted to play in the game and hoped to score a goal to dedicate it to Dinis. Unfortunately, the game finished in a 0–0 tie, and he was heartbroken that he was unable to score the goal for his father that day.

Trouble with a Teammate

Portugal did qualify for the World Cup, but there would be a personal cost for Ronaldo. Unfortunately the fierce competition between Portugal and England would result in a rift between him and some of his Manchester United teammates who were playing for England. So bitter was this rift, in fact, that it almost resulted in Ronaldo leaving MU.

The friction began during the quarter-final match between Portugal and England. Ronaldo's MU teammate Wayne Rooney was playing for England. In the sixty-second minute (games are ninety minutes long), Rooney stamped on Portugal's Ricardo Carvalho with his cleats. Furious at what he thought was a cheap shot, Ronaldo ran to the referee and complained that Rooney's actions were a cheap shot, and that he should receive a red card (meaning that he would have to leave the field and could not be substituted for, leaving England a man short). England's fans were furious that Ronaldo would lobby a referee to penalize Rooney, who was his teammate during the league season.

The referee did indeed issue a red card to Rooney. But Ronaldo added insult to injury when he walked on the field near England's team bench as Rooney made his way off the field. Ronaldo smiled and winked—which enraged the England fans even further. Later, in his book *My Decade in the Premier League,* Rooney says that while the fans were furious, he understood what Ronaldo was doing. "When I walked to the tunnel," he writes, "I knew I couldn't really blame Ronaldo for what had happened because he was trying to win the game for his country."[47]

As it turned out, Portugal won the game in a penalty shootout and reached its first semifinal World Cup match in forty years—losing to France 0–1.

Wayne Rooney of England stomps Ricardo Carvalho of Portugal during the FIFA World Cup quarter-final match on July 1, 2006. Cristiano Ronaldo's reaction to the serious offense angered some fans in England.

"We've Made Ronaldo's Wink the Bullseye"

But when the league season resumed, the MU fans had neither forgotten nor forgiven Ronaldo for the playful wink after he complained to the referee and urged him to kick Rooney out of the World Cup game. Even though he had been a contributing MU player, many fans now saw him as an enemy.

The media stoked the controversy, as well. The June 3, 2006, cover of *The Sun*, a UK tabloid, showed a picture of Ronaldo on a dartboard, with his winking eye in the bullseye. "Here's every England fan's chance to get revenge on the world's biggest winker. . . . We've made Ronaldo's wink the bullseye. So put it up in your office—and give the sly señor one in the eye."[48]

The booing and insults continued during the season, but Ferguson tried to soothe his young player, telling him that the fans would eventually forget the whole thing. Ronaldo said that he did not want to play if fans hated him. He asked to be traded to Real Madrid, which is closer to his home country of Portugal. Ferguson refused to let Ronaldo give up on Manchester United. The best thing, said the coach, is to ignore it and play the game. When Ronaldo threw himself into the game, Ferguson knew it would be impossible for MU fans to continue booing him. Ronaldo was simply too good.

Chapter 4

A Move to Spain

Predictably, Alex Ferguson was right, and Manchester United fans soon forgave Cristiano Ronaldo for the "winking incident." However, Ronaldo was thinking about changing teams. For a long time, he had been telling his agent that someday he would love to play with Real Madrid, the soccer team based in Spain's capital. In 2007, there were rumors that his time at MU

Cristiano Ronaldo waves to fans during his official presentation as a new member of Real Madrid at the Santiago Bernabeu stadium on July 6, 2009.

was soon coming to an end. The word was that his agent had worked out a way for Ronaldo to move to Real Madrid.

However, 2007 came and went, with Ronaldo still the key to Manchester United's offense. He insisted that he was in no hurry—he loved playing for MU. "Everyone knows I love Spain," he told reporters. "I would love to play there someday. But right now I'm happy at Man United. If I stay another two, three, four, five years, I'll be happy. It's a great club."[49]

In 2008, when the rumors began swirling again, Alex Ferguson was asked if he was bargaining to trade Ronaldo to the team in Spain; he did not hold back his annoyance. He was still furious that Real Madrid had been relentless in trying to sign Ronaldo during the season. "Do you think I would get into a contract with that mob [Real Madrid]?" he asked incredulously. "No chance. I wouldn't sell them a virus."[50]

80 Million Pounds

But a year later, on June 26, 2009, a joint statement from Real Madrid and Manchester United verified that finally the deal had been struck. Ronaldo had signed a six-year contract with Real Madrid and would start there just five days later, on July 1, 2009.

The amount of money paid by Real Madrid to Manchester United as a transfer fee was a staggering 80 million British pounds, or 121.2 million dollars. The actual salary Ronaldo would be making was 9.5 million pounds, the equivalent of 15.6 million dollars per year.

Wishing Ronaldo well, British Prime Minister Gordon Brown was nonethless disappointed that the star player would be leaving England, but was clear that there was no doubt that he was worth the extraordinary paycheck he would be earning. "He's one of the most brilliant players in the world. I think people will be sad that he's lost to the game in England."[51]

Doing Ads

Once he signed with Real Madrid, Ronaldo was also eager to continue a side venture that he had been pursuing since his

A Move to Spain **61**

Manchester United days—commercial endorsements. He actually did his first modeling ads when he was eighteen. The product was Pepe Jeans, a trademark of a London-based clothing company. He agreed to do it, he says, because it was a huge challenge—far different from anything he had ever done before.

"I saw it as another personal challenge, because I had to pose side by side with a professional model, who was used to the cameras, unlike me," he says, smiling:

> [The location] chosen was Barreiro, a Portuguese town near Lisbon and close to a factory area. It was a deserted wasteland that was ideal for the creation of some very stunning backdrops. . . . It was both curious and fun, although it took us two days of hard and tiring work. But it was worth it. At the end, the photographer told me that because of my calm attitude he could not believe this was my first time on a shoot.[52]

Playing Soccer with Ice Cubes

After those early advertisements, Ronaldo was sought after to do more endorsement work. One of the most fun experiences he had was doing a commercial for Coca-Cola that would be shown during the 2006 World Cup. He especially en-

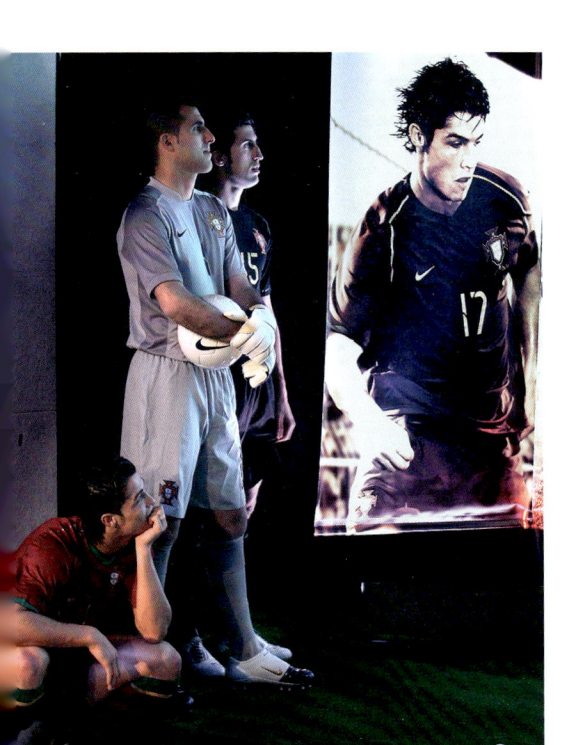

Portuguese national team members Cristiano Ronaldo, Ricardo Pereira, and Marco Caneira (left to right) watch a commercial promoting the team for the World Cup 2006.

joyed one in which he appeared to be inside a Coke can, doing fancy soccer moves such as bicycle kicks with ice cubes rather than soccer balls. He especially liked the last part of the commercial, when the Coke appeared to have come to life and hopped around making soccer moves.

One personal rule, he says, is important to him. He does ads only for products that he believes in or uses himself. He says that he does not need money badly enough to be talked into speaking for a product with which he is not familiar, or one that he does not really like.

Tons of Mail

Ronaldo receives thousands of letters from fans all around the world each week. When he first became a celebrity, he was charmed by the idea of getting so much mail. He says that because the fans are so supportive, he feels that he needs to acknowledge the mail he gets.

"At home I have one or two awards as best player resulting from a vote among the supporters," he says. "I feel I have the moral obligation to thank them. So to do this I now answer all these letters sent to me. I receive all kinds of requests, from autographs, to photos, shirts, birthday cards, or even money, believe it or not."[53]

He acknowledges that some of the requests border on the bizarre. In one of the letters contained in the boxes marked "requests," one fan wanted Ronaldo to finance his new business—a snail-breeding nursery. Others, aware that the soccer star is being paid a large salary for his athletic skills, send him their bank statements along with their mortgage or car payment stubs, hoping that he will pay them off!

Answering as Many as He Can

In his 2007 autobiography, *Moments,* Ronaldo explains that he tries to reserve one day each week to take care of correspondence that he receives from all over the world. His belief is that if fans care enough to write to him, he should at least

A Move to Spain

acknowledge their letters. It has become an expensive task. Though some correspondents include a self-addressed and stamped envelope, many do not. He says that in one month he spent more than 2,000 pounds (3,016 dollars) just on envelopes and stamps!

With the sheer numbers of letters, answering each one with a handwritten letter would be impossible, so he has asked his cousin Nuno and his friend Rogerio for their assistance in writing a short response. Nuno and Rogerio open the letters, get everything ready, and Ronaldo signs each letter.

"To answer the fans is one of my priorities," he says. "It is something I want to do. I have that obligation and will keep on doing it. I feel even more motivated and proud."[54]

A Slave to His Own Routines

Many of his fans do not realize how much he relies on tradition—doing the same things in the same way on every game day. Many athletes follow a specific regimen on game day—what they wear, what they eat, and even the order in which they put their clothes on. Whether these traditions are based on superstition or just his preferences, Ronaldo admits that he has a whole set of rules that make him feel more comfortable before each match.

For example, he must always put on his right sock first, just like the great Argentinian player Alfredo di Stefano. If he is not paying attention and puts on the left sock before the right, it will mean bad luck on the field that day. Just as crucial for Ronaldo

Cristiano Ronaldo brushes his hair with water—one of his pre-game routines—prior to a match in 2013.

Success in 2013

British sportswriter Sam Stevens listed Ronaldo's astonishing accomplishments during the 2013 season with Real Madrid:

Ronaldo's Incredible Numbers

> Ronaldo has outscored the Premier League's five biggest clubs in 2013.
> Ronaldo is the top scorer in the Champions League this season with eight goals.
> Ronaldo is the top scorer in La Liga this season with 16 goals in 13 matches.
> Ronaldo equaled Pauleta's national record of 47 goals for Portugal.
> Ronaldo has scored an incredible 66 goals for club and country in 2013. That includes 56 goals in 46 games for Real Madrid and 10 in nine for Portugal.
> Since joining Real Madrid, Ronaldo has scored 225 goals in 216 games for the club.

Sam Stevens. "Ronaldo's Incredible Numbers" in "In Ten Years He Has Gone from a Baby-Faced Lone Ranger to an Accomplished Killer . . . Forget Messi, Ibrahimovic, Ribery and the Rest, Ronaldo Is the Best Player in the World." *Daily Mail*, November 20, 2013. http://www.dailymail.co.uk/sport/football/article-2510768/Cristiano-Ronaldo-best-player-world-ahead-Lionel-Messi-Zlatan-Ibrahimovic-Franck-Ribery.html.

is the habit of stepping onto the field with the right foot; he also has a ritual of being the last in the line of his teammates. The only exception, note authors Luis Miguel Pereira and Juan Ignacio Gallardo, is when he is playing with the Portuguese National Team, because "he is the captain and therefore has to be the first one to enter the pitch [another word for the soccer field]."[55]

Even the way his hair looks during the game is important. He feels that it is bad luck to play more than ninety minutes with the same hairstyle, so he changes the style during halftime—often missing the conversation between the coach and players. There also are set habits that pertain only to the transportation to the stadium. He is the only player that sits in the back row of the bus and must be the last player to exit the bus when they arrive at the field.

Relaxing Before Matches

Once he is on the field in the moments before the game, Ronaldo says he follows another routine he has had since his earliest games as a young boy—playing around with a ball by himself. He tries to be the first of his team to arrive at his team's headquarters on each game day. He admits that he cannot help juggling the ball or simply tossing it from hand to hand:

> I used to do it when I played in the street, I kept on doing it all through my training and I still do it now. And I will keep doing it. This is the real Cristiano Ronaldo. I believe that when people see me on the pitch playing with the ball before the beginning of the warm-up period, they may be tempted to think that this is nothing but a charm offensive or showing off. If this is what you think then you are wrong, because I do it naturally.[56]

Ronaldo says that his ritual before the game—either a Real Madrid game or a Portuguese national team game—is always the same. He is very tense. As soon as the coach goes over the lineup for the day, he hurries to the dressing room and starts playing with the ball. Fans, he says, might be surprised as to why he does it:

> I take the ball, I pass it under one foot, and then the other, I pick it up, bounce it, in short, I amuse myself with the ball. I do it just for pleasure, but there is also another reason: to put an end to any tension I may have before the match. My teammates, in both the club and the Portuguese national team, can confirm this, as they know me very well. . . . I do not like to think much before a match and playing with the ball works as the perfect antidote.[57]

A Mystery Baby

If his fans are surprised that he is tense before matches, they were likely to have been flummoxed by off-the-field news that broke in the summer of 2010. On July 3, Ronaldo made an announcement on both Facebook and Twitter, saying that he had just become a father. However, there was a cloak of secrecy about the announcement that had his followers scratching their heads:

Cristiano Ronaldo Junior (left) and his father attend the Mutua Madrid Open tennis tournament on May 8, 2014.

It is with great joy and emotion that I inform I have recently become a father to a baby boy. As agreed with the baby's mother, who prefers to have her identity kept confidential, my son will be under my exclusive guardianship. No further information will be provided on this subject and I request everyone to fully respect my right to privacy (and that of the child) at least on issues as personal as these are.[58]

The news was perplexing, for twenty-year-old Ronaldo and his longtime girlfriend, model and actress Irina Shayk, had been seen together recently, and she had not looked at all pregnant. Not surprisingly, the tabloids were abuzz with rumors.

One reported that the baby was the result of a one-night stand with a twenty-year-old British woman who had no interest at all in raising the baby and, to keep her silence, had been paid a great deal of money. Another tabloid reported that Ronaldo had paid a young American woman from San Diego, California, to be a surrogate mother. According to that report, he had promised to pay her 16 million euros (18.6 million dollars) as long as she would give up her rights to the child and also to stay out of the press.

Six months later, a twenty-year-old British student told reporters that she was the mother of Ronaldo's son. She claimed to have received 10 million pounds (over 15 million dollars) from him to keep silent and to give up her rights to the child. In fact, according to the young woman, she was not even allowed to talk about the deal with her family members. She admitted that even though she was now living a millionaire's lifestyle, she felt guilty about agreeing to sever all ties with her child, and even guiltier because of the money she received for the deal.

Yet another explanation came from Katia, Ronaldo's sister. She discounted all of the rumors, telling reporters that the baby's mother had died. She refused to elaborate on how the little boy came into the world; however, she guaranteed that he was her brother's son. And luckily, she announced, her mother Dolores was excited to be a full-time caregiver, looking after her grandson.

No one seemed to know what to believe—or whom.

Cristiano Junior

The one indisputable fact was that as announced, the baby—named Cristiano Ronaldo Jr.—was in the care of Ronaldo's mother Dolores, in the home he bought for her in southern Portugal. Pictures published in the Portuguese magazine *TV Mais* showed the baby in Dolores's arms, with his face deliberately pixelated. But his skin tone and characteristics strongly resembled those of his father.

In December, Dolores took the baby to Bernabeu, the stadium where Real Madrid play their home games. Coincidentally, Ronaldo scored a goal, and pretending to suck on a pacifier, pointed up to his private box and waved. The cameras caught just a glimpse of the baby—for the first time. Since then, Ronaldo and his family have taken precautions that Cristiano Jr. is not photographed by the press, unless the family agrees to it first.

Soon after his son's outing at the soccer game, Ronaldo decided to be more open about his recent fatherhood in interviews with several European magazines. He claimed that becoming a father had made a big change in him, though he admitted that he was still learning. "Of course something like this affects you," he said. "It's a different type of responsibility. Maybe I feel more comfortable."

Asked if he changes diapers occasionally, he laughed. "It's not the thing I do best in the world," he said, "but I do it."[59]

Living Rich

It is not difficult to understand why anyone would be "very content" with the wealthy lifestyle Ronaldo enjoys. In 2015 *Forbes* magazine ranked him as the second-highest-paid athlete in the world. In addition to his annual 46-million-euro (52-million-dollar) salary, he earned 24 million euros (28 million dollars) in endorsements, including ones from Nike, Coca-Cola, and Armani.

He admits he loves to spend money—especially on his wardrobe. He estimates that he spends 8,000 pounds (12,900 dol-

Watches and Cars

Not only is Ronaldo generous with gifts to his family and friends, he is also willing to bestow gifts on teammates as a way of celebrating a joyous occasion. Real Madrid winning its tenth European Cup in 2013 was just such an occasion. The team celebrated its tenth European Cup win last season with Ronaldo scoring a late penalty in a 4–1 win over Atletico Madrid. Known as "La Decima" or "the tenth," it is a feat few teams have achieved.

The trophy success, coupled with Ronaldo's individual achievements, have prompted the Portuguese star to buy each and every one of his teammates a brand new gift—worth 8,200 euros (10,000 dollars) each. The Bulgari watch is engraved with the player's name, Ronaldo's initials, and shirt number "CR7." It also has the words "La Decima" engraved on the back, as a reminder of the squad's terrific accomplishment.

Not long after that, Ronaldo made a promise to bestow additional lavish gifts in the Real Madrid organization—this time to the physical therapists and doctors, depending on whether they kept him healthy enough during 2014 so he could win the coveted Ballon d'Or trophy. Ronaldo insisted that without the medics—those who do the physical therapy, the rubdowns after practices and games, and the massages that help relieve the aching muscles—he would not be nearly as successful as he has been. After he received the coveted trophy in January 2015, the medics had reason to celebrate.

lars) per month just on clothes. He also has purchased more than twenty automobiles—a virtual fleet—from a Bugatti Veyron sports car to a luxury Rolls-Royce Phantom.

He has invested in property, too. He owns nightclubs, a hotel, and various bars, which his brother runs. He has also indulged himself by building several houses, including a 5-million-pound (7.2-million-dollar) home where he lives in Madrid. It has seven bedrooms, two swimming pools, and beautiful gardens, and sits on more than an acre of land. Ronaldo admits that he even spent thousands of dollars having "CR7" etched in to the windows of his home and also emblazoned on his furnishings—from his sofa and dinner table to his dishes. "This is probably the most extravagant thing I've done,"[60] he says.

He does not scrimp at all when it comes to Cristiano Jr., either, though he insists that he does not want his son to become spoiled. "Although I was raised in poverty, he's going to be raised very rich," he says. "But I am not posh, so my son is not going to be posh. I don't want him to go to a posh school. I want him to mix with normal people."[61]

Ronaldo says that he is not ashamed to have been brought up poor, and he does not want his son to think that being wealthy is the only way to be happy. "I was brought up with nothing, we were very poor," he says.

> I had no toys and no Christmas presents. I shared a room with my brother and two sisters. . . . It was a small space. But I didn't mind. I'm incredibly close to my brother and two sisters and we loved being together. For us it was normal, it was all we knew. Everyone around us lived the same way and we were happy.[62]

Being Generous

He has certainly not been at all stingy with his money. In fact, one of the things of which he is most proud is being able to help his family and friends. He has paid for new homes for his sisters, as well as a beautiful house in Portugal for his mother.

He maintains that money has not changed him with regard to his choice of friends. "I have my circle of friends, my club," Ronaldo says. "People who've been with me a long time. I look after these people. I take them to five-star hotels. I pay for private planes. I pay at the bar. . . . I drink Red Bull while I buy my friends champagne at £1,000

Cristiano Ronaldo arrives at Manchester United's training grounds in 2008 driving a Bentley luxury coupe.

A Move to Spain   **73**

[$1,500] a bottle. It's no problem—I like my friends to be happy."⁶³

His generosity has not been limited to his friends and family. In 2014, a Spanish daily newspaper reported that Ronaldo had been approached by people holding a charity auction. The auction's purpose was to raise money for a ten-month-old boy, Erik Ortiz Cruz, to have a life saving operation. The baby had been diagnosed with cortical dysplasia, a dangerous brain condition that sometimes causes a sufferer to experience as many as thirty seizures per day.

The auction officials were trying to collect sports memorabilia that could be auctioned off to make money for the operation and wondered if Ronaldo would be willing donate a pair of his soccer cleats. He listened intently as the officials explained about the boy's condition and gave his answer. Rather than donate cleats, he said, he would be happy to pay for the operation and all of the treatments to follow.

He is not generous to gain popularity, he says. Rather, he is trying to do what his mother always taught him. "When I go home, my mom says: 'Son, you have done a good act in helping other people. It's good that you are interested in how the world lives.' It is so nice to hear things like that from people who are so important to me."⁶⁴

Chapter 5

Expanding His Reach

Besides being financially successful, Cristiano Ronaldo has continued to enjoy a great deal of success on the soccer field as well. So much, in fact, that he is considered by many to be the most talented player in the history of the sport. As a result, many scientists and sports analysts have wondered what it is that sets him apart from other highly skilled soccer players throughout the world.

In 2011, while part of the Real Madrid team, he agreed to be evaluated in several different experiments, helping scientists understand how he is able to perform the almost magical moves that look so easy for him on the soccer field. The experiments took place in Madrid, in a special state-of-the-art laboratory with the facilities that would enable them to put Ronaldo's abilities to the test. The astonishing results are explained in a documentary called *Ronaldo: Tested to the Limit*. The program shows how researchers evaluated his body strength, technique, and mental ability. What the scientists learned demonstrates just how uncommon an athlete Ronaldo is compared to others.

A Superbly Formed Body

The first part of the testing was evaluating his level of physical fitness. A physically demanding sport, soccer requires endurance, strength, and speed. The researchers painstakingly measured each of those variables, beginning with a 3-D body

Could Hexes Help?

Cristiano Ronaldo is arguably the most feared soccer player in the world because of his amazing scoring power—leaving defenders scratching their heads as he bobs and weaves around them and rifles the ball into the net for a goal. As a result, it seems that some opponents have resorted to unusual strategies to neutralize the superstar.

In June 2014, just days before Ronaldo's Portugal team was scheduled to play Ghana in the World Cup, a Ghanaian witch doctor, whose name translated into English means "The Devil of Wednesday," claimed that he put a hex on Ronaldo to prevent him from playing in the match. The hex, he says, caused Ronaldo to develop both tendon and muscle problems in his left knee and thigh, which forced him to miss a game with Greece.

"I said it four months ago that I will work on Cristiano Ronaldo seriously and rule him out of the World Cup or at least prevent him from playing against Ghana and the best thing I can do is to keep him out through injury," the witch doctor explained. "This injury can never be cured by any medic; they can never see what is causing the injury because it is spiritual," the witch doctor explained. "Today, it is his knee, tomorrow it is his thigh, next day it is something else."

The hex was only temporary, however, for Ronaldo scored the game-winning goal that led Portugal to defeat Ghana, 2–1.

Aileen Graef. "Ghanaian Witch Doctor Claims He Made Cristiano Ronaldo Injure His Knee." UPI Sports. June 5, 2014, in Business Source Premier.

scanner that uses laser beams to give exact measurements of his musculature. He has 3 percent less body fat than a supermodel, and because of his incredibly strong upper body and thighs, he is able to jump 2 feet, 6 inches (0.8 m)—higher than the average NBA player. That means that in a soccer game, he is able to head a ball that is more than 8 feet (2 m) off the ground.

Cristiano Ronaldo poses next to a poster for the documentary Cristiano Ronaldo: Tested to the Limit *in 2011.*

Expanding His Reach **77**

To see how his musculature helps him in sprinting ability, the scientists had him compete with a world-class champion sprinter, Angel Rodriguez. In the first test, a straight sprint of 82 feet (25 m), Rodriguez beat Ronaldo's time by only .3 seconds. But on the second sprint, a zigzag course—more typical of the type of running usually done in a soccer match, Ronaldo beat Rodriguez's time by .51 seconds.

Spatial Awareness

One of the next experiments was aimed at discovering the range of his mental and visual abilities that would affect him as a soccer player. He is exceptionally confident, he tells researchers. He always believes that he can be successful on the field, and that confidence helps him. "I always try to be focused in my game, and my mental ability is quite good,"[65] he says.

To understand the depth of those abilities, the researchers were especially interested in what he looks at while dribbling the ball as an opposing player is trying to steal it away from him—a scenario that occurs often during a match. To accurately see what Ronaldo's eyes are focused on, the researchers had the two players wear an eye-tracking apparatus. The scientists use a special infrared camera focused on the athletes' eyes, and that camera provides the researchers with the information they are processing visually.

What they found was very surprising. They expected that Ronaldo's eyes would frequently be focused on the ball he was trying to protect. On the contrary, the special cameras showed that he almost never looked at the ball. His almost instinctual ability to control the ball's movement means that only occasionally would he feel the need to glance down to see it. Instead, what he did look at was his opponent—from the movement of his hips, to the shifting of his feet—in order to predict which direction the opponent was going to move.

Those subtle cues provided him with a fraction of a second during which he could move in the other direction and prevent the ball from being stolen. For example, in one period of 8 seconds, Ronaldo was able to execute thirteen moves—including spins, feints, and step-overs—on his opponent. Those moves made it virtually impossible for his opponent to steal the ball. Meanwhile, the opponent's eyes were fixed on the ball almost all of the time—which did not seem to help him at all.

How does Ronaldo know how to make these split-second decisions? Sports psychologist Zoe Wimshurst, who oversaw the research, believes that it was the result of thousands of hours of playing soccer, from the time he was a young boy:

> He's effectively a scholar of football [soccer]. It's the same way of studying any other subject—learning a new language, for example. You learn basic rules of grammar, and different words. In football terms, that would be skills and then putting them into a match situation. When you become fluent in the language, you don't have to think about it as much.[66]

Changing the Conditions

Probably the most jaw-dropping of these research experiments was testing his abilities when the field condition is different from what he is accustomed to. Using an indoor soccer arena for this experiment, the researchers were curious as to how Ronaldo would do when visibility was virtually zero.

Wimshurst explained to Ronaldo what they were going to do: A soccer coach, Andy, feeds the ball in from the sideline, as though it is a cross during a real game, to a player who can kick or head the cross into the net. Ronaldo stands several yards outside the goal, about 30 yards (27 m) away from Andy, waiting for the cross. His aim—just as in a real game—is to score a goal either by heading or kicking the ball coming to him from Andy's cross. However, once the ball is in flight, she explains, the researchers will snap the lights off, and the stadium will be completely black.

"We're expecting you to put the ball in the goal," says Wimshurst. "We're hoping you'll have picked up some advance clues from Andy's body position; the shapes, the positioning of his feet and his hips, will tell you what will happen so you can get into the right position even though you can't see [the ball]."[67]

Tapping into His Memory Bank

To have a means of comparison, the researchers also asked an average-skilled amateur soccer player named Ronald to take part in the experiment. Ronald was approximately the same height and weight as Ronaldo. As Andy kicked the cross, the lights went out, and the entire stadium was plunged into total darkness. Ronald had absolutely no idea where the ball was, and laughed along later as the night-vision camera showed him leaping to do a header, but missing the ball by yards.

When Ronaldo's turn came, the researchers all heard a "thud," evidence that he at least made contact with the ball. When the lights went on, they were astonished to see that Ronaldo had headed the ball into the goal. He did it again in darkness, this time kicking it into the goal, since he correctly predicted that Andy's cross kick would be too low to be headed into the goal. The scientists as well as the camera and sound crew applauded what seemed to be an impossible feat.

The experiment became more difficult in the next stage. This time, the lights were switched off at the exact moment Andy's foot connected with the ball. Amateur player Ronald, who had had no success before, was even more confounded. But Ronaldo was able to connect with both tries, getting two goals.

The results were amazing, but the real question was, how could Ronaldo have connected successfully with the ball numerous times, with the stadium in complete darkness? Wimshurst calculated that in just 500 milliseconds, Ronaldo's subconscious had interpreted Andy's body language, calculated the speed and trajectory of Andy's kick, and programmed his own body to reach it at the best moment for successfully making contact and getting the goal.

He is able to make such lightning-fast calculations by tapping into his memory banks, she explains,

> from thousands of hours of practice, which has filled his mind with so many permutations of the game to tap into, that when it comes to match play he has an uncanny ability to perform without having to think or look at the ball. . . . It's almost as if he is doing the math in his head.[68]

Museu CR7

In December 2013, Ronaldo embarked on yet another venture—a museum dedicated to his soccer career. With hundreds of medals, trophies, awards, and other memorabilia connected with his years of competitive soccer, he thought it was a good idea to allow the public to get a close-up look. He decided to call it the Museu (Portuguese for "museum") CR7.

The museum was actually the brainstorm of his brother, Hugo, who still lives in the city of Funchal on the island of Madeira. Hugo had gone to visit Ronaldo in Madrid after his brother

Museu CR7 features a wax statue of Cristiano Ronaldo and memorabilia from his athletic career. The museum opened in 2013 in the main tourist area of Ronaldo's hometown, Funchal, on the island of Madeira.

Expanding His Reach

A Mysterious Juggler

It was a chilly day in January 2015, in Madrid, Spain's capital, but people still gathered in the streets, some sitting at outdoor café tables, others in groups outside shops chatting. All of a sudden, a bespectacled, heavyset man—likely a homeless beggar—with long hair and a beard stepped forward. He took out a soccer ball from a backpack and began juggling it, using his feet and his head to keep it airborne. The people nearby began to watch, impressed that a man who was clearly so out of shape could do such athletic moves. It seemed that surely he would probably get some donations for a bowl of soup or a cup of coffee for the demonstration he was putting on.

One of the most interested was a young boy in a blue jacket. He seemed mesmerized by the juggling, and shyly moved closer to the man and watched more intently. As the minutes went by with the ball under complete and total control, the heavyset beggar suddenly stopped, catching the ball neatly. People applauded, and the man smiled and removed what was actually a wig and a beard! He then took off his glasses, and everyone gasped. It was Cristiano Ronaldo, having a little fun in a fat suit, pretending to be a homeless beggar. He bent down to hug the boy in the blue jacket, and talked with fans who crowded around him before leaving.

began playing with the Real Madrid team. Hugo shook his head in disbelief when he saw trophies and plaques and commemorations scattered around his brother's house. He suggested that they organize it and put it on display.

Coincidentally, a few years before, Ronaldo had purchased a five-story building near Funchal harbor, hoping to turn it into either a restaurant or a disco. But now, the brothers agreed, it would make an excellent location for the museum. With his iconic "CR7" logo spelled out in black tiles on the floor of the museum, the rooms are spacious—filled with gleaming white shelves displaying his trophies and medals. There is a life-sized wax statue of Ronaldo and an interactive game where any of the one thousand visitors per week are welcome to try to outplay him in heading a ball.

From the little gold cup he won at age eight, playing for Andorinha, to the FIFA Ballon d'Or presented to him in 2013 and again in 2014 as the best player in the world, visitors to the museum can see everything Ronaldo has accomplished—at least, so far. But Ronaldo says the museum is a work in progress. "I have room for more trophies,"[69] he insists.

Underwear, Rosaries, and Eyeglasses

In addition to his museum, Ronaldo has expanded his reach by adding fashion lines to his list of projects. For years he had been interested in men's fashions and enjoyed dressing with style in mind. Instead of appearing in public in a T-shirt and

Cristiano Ronaldo's CR7 store in Funchal, Madeira, features fashion accessories designed by Ronaldo himself and other items with a Cristiano Ronaldo theme.

Expanding His Reach **83**

blue jeans, as he did when he first went to England, he often prefers dressing more stylishly—wearing suits and fitted dress shirts and almost always sporting rather large diamond earrings. Because of his celebrity status, he found that his style has caught on with other young men.

Starting in 2008, he teamed up with designers to create belt buckles, shoes, dress shirts, underwear, and colorfully striped socks—all clearly marked with his now-iconic CR7. Because he is a devout Catholic, he even ordered five thousand rosaries with the CR7 mark and sold them through his online stores.

Another of the unusual items sold by Ronaldo's stores has been something that he himself wears, but does not need—eyeglasses. His vision is perfect, so why is he frequently seen wearing horn-rimmed or black-rimmed glasses with non-prescription lenses? The answer, simply, is that he likes the look—and evidently so do customers who have bought CR7 glasses.

Does Being Fashionable Make Him Healthier?

Ronaldo has long enjoyed fashion, although he insists that he rarely conforms to other people's ideas on what looks good. He prefers to set his own trends. Interestingly, however, this need to make himself look good is not entirely motivated by ego or narcissism.

In fact, it was one of the Real Madrid team doctors who shared his philosophy with Ronaldo—that the better one feels about oneself, the stronger one's self-esteem. The doctor explained to him, "We know that having a good self-image strengthens the immune system and prevents disease, and that is very important from the point of view of physical activity and athletic performance."[70]

In writing their book *The Secrets of the Machine,* Luis Miguel Pereira and Juan Ignacio Gallardo found that "this is the absolute truth as regards Cristiano, whose self-esteem increases his motivation, stimulates his will to train, and defines higher marks and targets."[71]

Feuding with a Rival

But while he has been successful at his fashion business and hailed by many soccer enthusiasts as the best player in the world, Ronaldo says he still feels that he has some things left to prove. One thing that has continued to rankle him is his ongoing competition with another soccer superstar—Lionel (often called Leo, for short) Messi. Both men play in what is known as La Liga (Spanish for "the League"), the top league

Cristiano Ronaldo (left) and Lionel Messi—both nominees for the 2013 Player of the Year Award—participate in a press conference prior to the Ballon d'Or ceremony in Zurich, Switzerland.

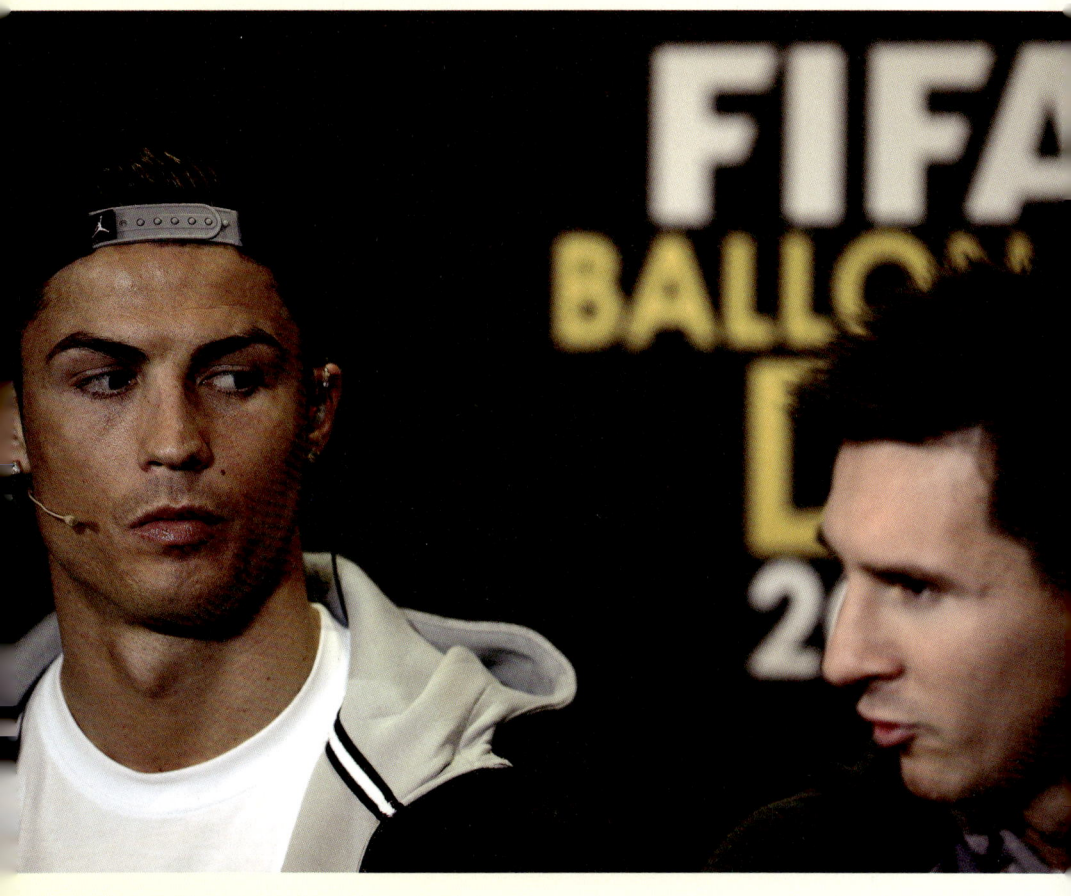

Expanding His Reach 85

made up of twenty teams in the Spanish Football League System. While Ronaldo plays for Real Madrid, Messi plays for FC Barcelona.

Luca Caioli, who has written biographies of both men, repeats a joke that has been very popular online. Caioli says that it illustrates how soccer fans view the rivalry between the two highly talented and amazingly egocentric athletes: "Two footballers are sitting on a sofa, chatting. 'God sent me down to Earth to teach people how to play football,' says Cristiano Ronaldo. 'Don't be daft, I didn't send anyone down to Earth,' replies Messi."[72]

It's easy to see why Ronaldo and Messi are brimming with self-confidence. They are the two most highly paid soccer players in history. Between them, they have six World Player of the Year titles. But there are also big differences between Messi and Ronaldo, especially in their personalities. Sepp Blatter, the current president of FIFA, the Federation Internationale de Football Association, offered his opinion on how differently the two players present themselves: "Lionel Messi is a good boy who every mother and father would like to have at home," he said. "He's a good man . . . he's a kind man . . . and that's what makes him so popular." But Blatter did not stop there. "One [meaning Ronaldo] has more expenses for the hairdresser than the other. I like both of them, but I prefer Messi."[73]

There is no doubt that Ronaldo is outwardly more confident—many would characterize him as arrogant. Many soccer traditionalists ridicule him for his striking good looks, his devotion to fashion, his outspoken nature, and even the enormous paychecks he earns. Sometimes it seems as if he goes out of his way to invite criticism, such as in 2013, when he was asked why crowds often jeered him. He thought about it for a moment and answered matter-of-factly, "I think that because I'm rich, handsome, and a great player, people are envious of me. I don't have any other explanation."[74]

In his autobiography, former Manchester United coach Alex Ferguson offers his opinion of the two men's attributes. "Ronaldo's got a better physique than Messi," he says. "He's better in the air, he's got two feet [equally capable of scoring goals] and he's quicker. [But] Messi has something magical about him when the ball touches his feet. It's as if it's landed on a bed of feathers. His low sense of gravity is devastating."[75]

The 2014 Ballon d'Or

The one measuring stick used in naming the best player in the world for a particular year is a trophy called the Ballon d'Or (Golden Ball). It is an award that has special meaning because the winner is selected by team coaches and captains, as well as journalists. Over the previous four years, Messi had won it three times and Ronaldo once, in 2013.

But 2014 was a very successful year for Ronaldo. He scored an astonishing total of sixty-one goals. His Real Madrid

Cristiano Ronaldo poses with his 2013 Ballon d'Or trophy on January 13, 2014.

team won its tenth European Cup title in La Liga, known as "La Decima" or "the tenth." On January 12, 2015, it was announced that Cristiano Ronaldo had been selected the winner of the 2014 FIFA Ballon d'Or. Jubilant over winning the trophy, he expressed his gratitude to all of those who voted for him. He also vowed that his goal was to continue to improve, because he had a lofty ambition. "I want to keep challenging myself every day," he said. "I want to become one of the greatest players of all time. Of course, this requires effort but I hope to get there."[76]

Ronaldo also explained that he believed the rivalry that existed between Messi and himself was actually a good thing for both of them. "I'm sure that the competition between us is a motivating factor for him, too," he said. "It's good for me, for him, and for other players that are keen to grow."[77]

Diamonds on His Shoes

Within days of winning the Ballon d'Or in January 2015, Nike announced that it had designed a special set of soccer cleats just for Ronaldo. The shoes are named "Mercurial CR7 Rare Gold" boots, or "Nike CR7s" for short. The shoes are gold in color and have what are known as "micro-diamonds" fastened and stitched into the shoes.

Obviously, the shoes are one-of-a-kind, just as Nike says Cristiano Ronaldo is: an incredible athlete with a "remorseless work ethic."[78] The company explained that they intend the micro-diamonds to be actually symbolic of the way he trains and perfects his abilities on the field:

> The micro-diamonds are remnants from larger stones that are painstakingly perfected by craftsmen. As the diamonds are refined and the details sharpened, tiny pieces are cut away, leaving micro-diamonds behind as evidence of work in progress. The commitment to keep chipping away at something already impressive reminded Nike's design team of Ronaldo's work ethic. While many see Ronaldo as the best in the world, he sees room for improvement.[79]

Cristiano Ronaldo wears personalized CR7 Nike boots with pink studs during a game in Germany in February 2015.

How Long Can He Play?

As of 2015, Ronaldo is under contract with Real Madrid until 2018. Other clubs have made offers to him, but he insists that he is happy in Madrid and is glad to continue to play international games with Portugal's national team. One name continues to come up—Manchester United. He enjoyed his time in the Premier League in England and has maintained his close friendship with coach Alex Ferguson.

His longtime agent, Jorge Mendes, is fairly confident that Ronaldo will finish out his career with Real Madrid—which could be another seven or eight years, since his thirty-year-old client is in such top form. "I'm almost certain he'll retire at 38 or 39," says Mendes, "because he's got a lot of years in him yet. We all know he's a total professional, the kind of person that really looks after himself."[80]

Expanding His Reach

As for Ronaldo, in 2015 he is evidently at the top of his game. He's got a son whom he adores and a devoted family. Life has been good to him, and he is happy doing what he does best. His millions of fans around the world are grateful to have the chance to experience the magic he creates on the soccer field.

Notes

Introduction: "The Very, Very Best in the World"

1. Quoted in Tim Lewis. "Cristiano Ronaldo: He's Got a God-Given Talent—and He Knows It." *The Guardian*. November 23, 2013. http://www.theguardian.com/the observer/2013/nov/24/cristiano-ronaldo-real-madrid-portugal-football.
2. Sky Sports. Portugal vs. Sweden, televised game. November 19, 2013.
3. Quoted in Lewis. "Cristiano Ronaldo."
4. Sky Sports. Portugal vs. Sweden, televised game.

Chapter 1: An Island Childhood

5. Quoted in Luca Caioli. *Ronaldo: The Obsession for Perfection*. London: Corinthian Books, 2012, p. 11.
6. Cristiano Ronaldo with Manuela Brandao. *Moments*. London: Macmillan, 2007, p. 48.
7. Ronaldo. *Moments*, p. 48.
8. Quoted in Caioli. *Ronaldo,* p. 11.
9. Ronaldo. *Moments*, p. 18.
10. Ronaldo. *Moments*, p. 18.
11. Ronaldo. *Moments,* pp. 18, 23.
12. Quoted in Caioli. *Ronaldo,* p. 11.
13. Roberto Navarro, personal interview with the author. December 2, 2014. Minneapolis, MN.
14. Ronaldo. *Moments*, p. 23.
15. Ronaldo. *Moments*, p. 23.
16. Quoted in Caioli. *Ronaldo,* p. 13.
17. Quoted in Caioli. *Ronaldo,* p. 14.
18. Quoted in Goal.com. March 30, 2012. http://www.goal.com/en/news/1717/editorial/2012/03/30/2997825/he-was-sobbing-like-a-child-whose-favourite-toy-had-been.
19. Quoted in Tom Oldfield. *Cristiano Ronaldo: The £80*

Million Man—The Inside Story of the Greatest Footballer on Earth. London: John Blake, 2007, pp. 14–15.
20. Caioli. *Ronaldo*, p. 14.

Chapter 2: Club Soccer

21. Quoted in Caioli. *Ronaldo*, p. 15.
22. Quoted in Caioli. *Ronaldo*, p. 16.
23. Quoted in Caioli. *Ronaldo*, p. 16.
24. Quoted in Luis Miguel Pereira and Juan Ignacio Gallardo. *CR7: The Secrets of the Machine*. Estoril, Portugal: Prime, 2014 (e-book), chapter 2.
25. Quoted in Caioli. *Ronaldo*, p. 19.
26. Quoted in Caioli. *Ronaldo*, p. 20.
27. Ronaldo. *Moments*, p. 56.
28. Ronaldo. *Moments*, p. 56.
29. Pereira and Gallardo. *CR7: Secrets of the Machine*, chapter 2.
30. Quoted in Caioli. *Ronaldo*, p. 21.
31. Quoted in Caioli. *Ronaldo*, p. 35.
32. Pereira and Gallardo. *CR7: The Secrets of the Machine*, chapter 1.
33. Quoted in Jay Mize. "What Does World Cup Star Cristiano Ronaldo and Children's Medical Center Have in Common?" Children's Health Blog, June 19, 2014. http://blog.childrens.com/what-does-world-cup-star-cristiano-ronaldo-and-childrens-medical-center-have-in-common.
34. Quoted in "Ronaldo's Career Rescued by Heart Op." The Nation. January 30, 2009. http://thenationonlineng.net/archive2/tblnews_Detail.php?id=76036.

Chapter 3: The Most Expensive Teenager in Britain

35. Caioli. *Ronaldo*, p. 29.
36. Pereira and Gallardo. *CR7: Secrets of the Machine*, chapter 2.
37. Quoted in Caioli. *Ronaldo*, p. 38.
38. Quoted in Caioli. *Ronaldo*, p. 42.
39. Quoted in Oldfield. *Cristiano Ronaldo*, p. 23.

40. Dan Taylor. "Teenager Takes Beckham No7 Shirt." *The Guardian*. August 13, 2003. http://www.theguardian.com/football/2003/aug/13/newsstory.sport10.
41. Quoted in Caioli. *Ronaldo*, p. 46.
42. Ronaldo. *Moments*, p. 61.
43. Quoted in Oldfield. *Cristiano Ronaldo*, p. 33.
44. Quoted in Oldfield. *Cristiano Ronaldo*, p. 33.
45. Ronaldo. *Moments*, p. 61.
46. Quoted in Caioli. *Ronaldo*, pp. 62–63.
47. Quoted in "Rooney on . . . Ronaldo: The Truth Behind That Wink and My Red Card." Mirror Online. September 9, 2012. http://www.mirror.co.uk/sport/football/news/wayne-rooney-exclusive-on-cristiano-ronaldo-1314153.
48. Quoted in Caioli. *Ronaldo*, p. 83.

Chapter 4: A Move to Spain

49. Quoted in Caioli. *Ronaldo*, p. 117.
50. Quoted in Steve Wilson. "Sir Alex Ferguson 'Wouldn't Sell Real Madrid a Virus,' Let Alone Cristiano Ronaldo." *The Telegraph*. December 18, 2008. http://www.telegraph.co.uk/sport/football/teams/manchester-united/3832913/Sir-Alex-Ferguson-wouldnt-sell-Real-Madrid-a-virus-let-alone-Cristiano-Ronaldo.html.
51. Quoted in Caioli. *Ronaldo*, p. 113.
52. Ronaldo. *Moments*, pp. 30–31.
53. Ronaldo. *Moments*, p. 79.
54. Ronaldo. *Moments*, p. 79.
55. Pereira and Gallardo. *CR7: The Secrets of the Machine*, chapter 5.
56. Ronaldo. *Moments*, p. 39.
57. Ronaldo. *Moments*, p. 39.
58. Quoted in Caioli. *Ronaldo*, p. 174.
59. Quoted in "'Of Course I Change Nappies': Cristiano Ronaldo Opens up About Fatherhood." *Hello Magazine*. January 20, 2011. http://us.hellomagazine.com/celebrities/201101204819/cristiano-ronaldo/baby/nappies/.
60. Quoted in "Cristiano Ronaldo Spills All to His 'Close Friend' Jasmine About Women, Football, Cars . . . and

Money." July 3, 2011. Mirror Online. http://www.mirror.co.uk/3am/celebrity-news/cristiano-ronaldo-spills-all-to-his-close-friend-139054.

61. Quoted in "Cristiano Ronaldo Spills All."
62. Quoted in "Cristiano Ronaldo Spills All."
63. Quoted in "Cristiano Ronaldo Spills All."
64. Quoted in Kevin Baxter. "Charity Is Nothing New for Cristiano Ronaldo." *Los Angeles Times.* May 17, 2014. http://www.latimes.com/sports/la-sp-wc-cristiano-ronaldo-20140518-story.html.

Chapter 5: Expanding His Reach

65. Quoted in *Cristiano Ronaldo: Tested to the Limit.* https://www.youtube.com/watch?v=vSL-gPMPVXI.
66. Quoted in *Cristiano Ronaldo: Tested to the Limit.*
67. Quoted in *Cristiano Ronaldo: Tested to the Limit.*
68. Quoted in *Cristiano Ronaldo: Tested to the Limit.*
69. Quoted in Alice Jones. "Inside Cristiano Ronaldo's Museum: 'I Have Room for More Trophies.'" *The Independent.* February 25, 2014. http://www.independent.co.uk/sport/football/news-and-comment/inside-cristiano-ronaldos-museum-i-have-room-for-more-trophies-9152637.html.
70. Quoted in Pereira and Gallardo. *CR7: The Secrets of the Machine*, chapter 5.
71. Pereira and Gallardo. *CR7: The Secrets of the Machine*, chapter 5.
72. "Messi Is Like Kryptonite to Cristiano Ronaldo's Superman: The Story Behind Football's Greatest Modern Rivalry." Goal.com. April 20, 2012. http://www.goal.com/en-gb/news/3277/la-liga/2012/04/20/3048281/messi-is-like-kryponite-to-cristiano-ronaldos-superman-the-story-.
73. Quoted in Tim Lewis. "Cristiano Ronaldo: He's Got a God-Given Talent—and He Knows It." *The Guardian.* November 23, 2013. http://lewis324.rssing.com/chan-10343783/all_p5.html.
74. Quoted in Jamie Jackson. "Cristiano Ronaldo: I'm Booed Because I'm Rich, Handsome, and Brilliant." *The*

Guardian. September 15, 2011. http://www.theguardian.com/football/2011/sep/15/cristiano-ronaldo-booed-rich-handsome.

75. Quoted in Jonathan Liew. "Cristiano Ronaldo and Lionel Messi Look Human but They Are Superheroes—Don't Compare Them, Just Appreciate." *The Telegraph*. October 23, 2014. http://www.telegraph.co.uk/sport/football/players/cristiano-ronaldo/11182468/Cristiano-Ronaldo-and-Lionel-Messi-look-human-but-they-are-superheroes-dont-compare-them-just-appreciate.html.

76. Quoted in "Ronaldo Aiming to Become One of 'Greatest Players of All Time.'" BreakingNews.ie. January 13, 2015. http://www.breakingnews.ie/sport/other/ronaldo-aiming-to-become-one-of-greatest-players-of-all-time-657838.html.

77. "Cristiano Ronaldo: Rivalry with Lionel Messi Motivates Both Players." ESPN FC. January 20, 2015. http://www.espnfc.com/spanish-primera-division/story/2254941/cristiano-ronaldo-says-rivalry-with-lionel-messi-motivates-both-players.

78. Quoted in Chris Wright. "Cristiano Ronaldo to Wear Diamond-Encrusted 'CR7' Boots." ESPN FC. January 13, 2015. http://www.espnfc.com/blog/the-toe-poke/65/post/2241625/cristiano-ronaldo-to-wear-goldendiamond-encrusted-cr7-boots.

79. Quoted in Brooks Peck. "Cristiano Ronaldo to Wear Diamond-Encrusted Gold Boots to Celebrate Third Ballon d'Or." Dirty Tackle. January 12, 2015. http://www.dirtytackle.net/2015/01/12/cristiano-ronaldo-to-wear-diamond-encrusted-gold-boots-to-celebrate-third-ballon-dor/.

80. Quoted in "I'm Convinced CR7 Will Retire at Real Madrid." Marca.com. January 22, 2015. http://www.marca.com/en/2015/01/22/en/football/real_madrid/1421967505.html.

Important Dates

1985
Cristiano Ronaldo dos Santos Aveiro is born on February 5, in Funchal, on the Portuguese island of Madeira.

1994
Nine-year-old Ronaldo joins his first football team in Funchal.

1997
Ronaldo goes with his godfather to the mainland to try out for Sporting Lisbon.

2001
On September 1, at the age of sixteen, Ronaldo is promoted to Sporting's senior team, giving him the status of a professional player.

2003
Ronaldo is transferred from Sporting Lisbon to Manchester United.

2005
Ronaldo wins an award (voted on by fans) for best young football player in the world.

2005
On September 5, Ronaldo learns that his father, Dinis, has died.

2006
Ronaldo and his Portugal Nacional team beat England's team in the European Cup match, eventually causing friction with Manchester United fans.

2007
Ronaldo wins the trophy for England's Best Player of the Year for his performance with Manchester United.

2009

In July Ronaldo is transferred from Manchester United to Real Madrid.

2010

Ronaldo announces that he is the proud father of a baby boy, Cristiano Jr.

2013

In December he opens the Museu CR7 in his hometown of Funchal.

2014

Ronaldo wins his second Ballon d'Or, the coveted trophy awarded to the male player whose play was deemed the best in the previous year.

For More Information

Books

Luca Caoli. *Messi, Neymar, Ronaldo: Head to Head With the World's Greatest Players.* London: Icon Books, 2014. An interesting book that focuses on three of the most interesting players today—from their childhoods to their unique abilities.

Tom Oldfield. *Cristiano Ronaldo: The £80 Million Man—The Inside Story of the Greatest Footballer on Earth.* London: John Blake, 2007. This book has an excellent section on Ronaldo's teen years, and his time with Manchester United.

Luis Miguel Pereira and Juan Ignacio Gallardo. *CR7: The Secrets of the Machine.* Estoril, Portugal: Prime Books, 2014. This e-book provides details about Ronaldo's life as well as how he trains and prepares.

Cristiano Ronaldo with Manuela Brandao. *Moments.* London: Macmillan, 2007. This book provides beautiful photographs and interesting sections on his interest in marketing and advertising, as well as helpful information on his difficult time with Sporting Lisbon.

Periodicals and Internet Sources

"The Fittest Man Alive." *Men's Health,* July 29, 2014. http://www.menshealth.com/fitness/fittest-man-alive.

Jamie Jackson. "Cristiano Ronaldo: I'm Booed Because I'm Rich, Handsome and Brilliant." *The Guardian,* September 15, 2011. http://www.theguardian.com/football/2011/sep/15/cristiano-ronaldo-booed-rich-handsome.

James Orr. "Cristiano Ronaldo Pays €60,000 for Brain Operation for 10-Month-Old Boy." *The Independent,* March 12, 2014, http://www.independent.co.uk/sport/football/european/cristiano-ronaldo-paying-60000-for-brain-operation-for-10monthold-boy-9187412.html.

"Ronaldo, Messi Continue Game of One-Upmanship," Fox Sports, January 18, 2015. http://www.foxsports.com/soccer

/story/cristiano-ronaldo-lionel-messi-rivalry-duel-la-liga
-stars-011815.

Websites

Cristiano Ronaldo's Fan Page (www.ronaldo7.net) This site contains chat rooms where fans debate, for example, whether Cristiano Ronaldo should leave Real Madrid and return to Manchester United, or the validity of recent penalties he has received. This site also contains photos and biographical information.

Cristiano Ronaldo's Official Website (www.cristianoronaldo.com) This site contains statistics, lots of photographs, and a helpful career timeline. It also includes a fan wall, where Ronaldo's many supporters can post videos, messages, and photos.

Manchester United's Cristiano Ronaldo Page (http://www.manutd.com/en/Players-And-Staff/Legends/Cristiano-Ronaldo.aspx) Though he left the team years ago, Ronaldo was such a fan favorite that his fan page still gets plenty of attention. His statistics as well as information about the team can be found here.

Real Madrid's Cristiano Ronaldo Page (http://www.realmadrid.com/en/football/squad/cristiano-ronaldo-dos-santos) This is a one-page introduction to Ronaldo, including quotations, a brief history of his time with Real Madrid, and statistics—from the number of minutes played so far this season to the assists and goals he has made.

Index

A
"Abelhinha" (Little Bee) (nickname), 19, 23–24
Afonso, Francisco, 22–23
Aveiro, Jose Dinis (father)
  alcoholism, 40–41
  Andorinha, soccer club, 15, 22
  death of, 55
  love of soccer, 15
  overview, 11–12
Aveiro, Maria Dolores dos Santos (mother)
  approval of soccer, 20
  concerns for son, 26, 48
  frustration over soccer, 19–20
  as grandmother, 69–70
  overview, 11–12

B
Ballon d'Or (Golden Ball) trophy, 87, 87–88
Beckham, David, 49, 50

C
Campeonato Brasileiro Série A, 45
Cardoso, Paulo, 28, 30
Carvalho, Ricardo, 57, 58
Commercial endorsements, 61–63
Competitive spirit, 29, 81
CR7 store, 83, 83–84
Cruz, Erik Ortiz, 74
"Crybaby" (nickname), 23, 32–35

E
Early childhood
  attention from scouts, 24–25
  attracting attention, 24–25
  birthplace, 14
  futebol, discovering, 14–16
  home life, 11–13
  lure of soccer, 18–20
  practicing, 22
  soccer vs. school, 17, 17–18, 20–22
English Premier League, 45

F
Family death, 55–57, 56

Fan mail, 63–64
Ferguson, Sir Alex, 21, 46, 46–47, 59, 61, 86–87
Freitas, Joao Marques, 28
Funchal (Madeira, Portugal), 11–13, 12–13, 24
Futebol, discovering, 14–16

H
Heart rhythm concerns, 36–37, *37*
Hugo (brother), 40, 81–82

I
Ibrahimovic, Zlatan, 8
Injuries, *33*, 76
International attention, 43–46, *44*

M
Major League Soccer (MLS), 45
Manchester United (MU)
  debut with, 50–51, *51*
  fan controversy, 58–59
  first impressions, 21, 48–50, *49*
  signing with, 46–47
  starting with, 47–48
  teammate troubles, 57, *58*
  unexpected honor under, 52
Maritimo, soccer club, 24–25
Martunis (earthquake survivor), 52–55, *54*
Memory bank tests, 80
Mendoca, Antonio, 26, 27
"Mercurial CR7 Rare Gold" boots, 88, *89*
Messi, Lionel, 6, *85*, 85–86
Moments (Ronaldo), 63
Moving from home, 30–32
Museu CR7, *81*, 81–83

N
Nacional da Madeira, soccer club
  attention from scouts, 24–25
  competitive spirit, 29
  new player evaluation, 26–27, *27*
  tryouts, 28
New player evaluation, 26–27, *27*
Nistelrooy, Ruud van, 21–22

P

Pereira, Aurelio, 30, 35

Personal life
  as father, 68, 68–70
  generosity, 71, 73–74
  living rich, 70–73, 72–73

Practicing
  early childhood, 18, 21–22
  physical therapy after, 71
  thousands of hours of, 80

R

Real Madrid years
  accomplishments under, 66
  commercial endorsements, 61–63
  desire to be traded to, 59
  ending career with, 89
  establishing routines under, 64–67, 64–65
  fan mail, 63–64
  pre-match relaxation, 67
  trade to, 59, *60*, 60–61

Rodriguez, Angel, 78

Rooney, Wayne, 57, 58

S

Scolari, Luiz Felipe, 55

Silva, Osvaldo, 28, 30

Skills, scientific evaluation
  changing conditions, 79
  memory bank, 80
  overview, 75
  physical fitness, 75–78, *77*
  self-esteem, 84
  spatial awareness, 78–79
  years left in the game, 89–90

Sousa, Fernao, 14–15, 24–25, 28

Southeast Asian earthquake, 52–55, *54*

Sporting Lisbon years
  catheter ablation, 38
  consequences for misbehavior, 35–36
  "crybaby" (nickname), 23, 32–35
  demanding nature of, *31*, 32
  growing confidence under, 42–43
  heart rhythm concerns, 36–37, *37*
  infractions incurred, 34

international attention,
  43–46, *44*
moving from home,
  30–32
opportunities under,
  38–40, *39*
signing with, 30
tryout for, 28

W
World Cup (2006), 7, 62
World Cup (2014), 7, 76
World Cup Qualifying
  match, 6–10, 7, *9*
World Player of the Year
  titles, 86

Picture Credits

Cover: © Victor Fraile/Corbis Sports/Corbis
© Alex Livesey/Getty Images, 58
© Antonio Cotrim/EPA/Newscom, 39
© Carlos Alvarez/Getty Images, 77
© Carlos Manuel Martins/ZUMA Press/Newscom, 20
© Christof Koepsel/Bongarts/Getty Images, 27
© CityFiles/WireImage/Getty Images, 33
© Eric Estrade/AFP/Getty Images, 44
© Europa Press/Europa Press via Getty Images, 68
© Fabrice Coffrini/AFP/Getty Images, 87
© Francisco Leong/AFP/Getty Images, 7
© Francisco Paraiso/AFP/Getty Images, 54
© Gonzalo Arroyo Moreno/Getty Images, 64–65
© Gregorio Cunha/AFP/Getty Images, 14, 17
© John Peters/Manchester United via Getty Images, 46
© Jose Sena Goulao/EPA/Newscom, 24
© Kieran McManus/BPI/REX/Newscom, 89
© Nicolas Asfouri/AFP/Getty Images, 62
© Olaf Protze/LightRocket via Getty Images, 12–13
© Oliver Morin/AFP/Getty Images, 85
© Pierre-Philippe Marcou/AFP/Getty Images, 60
© Pontus Lundahl/AFP/Getty Images, 9
© Richard Pasley/Doctor Stock/Getty Images, 37
© Splash News/Newscom, 72–73
© VI Images via Getty Images, 31

About the Author

Gail B. Stewart is an award-winning author of more than 180 books for children, teens, and young adults. She lives in Minneapolis with her husband. They are the parents of three grown sons.

Wake Technical Community College
9101 Fayetteville Road
Raleigh, North Carolina 27603

DATE DUE